Glasgow
and surrounding area

Travel Publications

CONTENTS

INTRODUCTION

A thousand years have been here and gone;
Since Kentigern saw the banks of Clyde;
But how many dreams and how many tears;
In the thousand years of a city's life;
A city hard a city proud;
No mean city it has been;
Perhaps tomorrow it yet may be;
The Dear Green Place again...

The City of Glasgow, Scotland's most populous city with three-quarters of a million inhabitants, has a long-established tradition as an important industrial centre and major port. It is now also enjoying a growing reputation as a cultural centre, stemming from its reputation for innovative architecture, art and design.

■ Geography
Situation

Situated in the west of Scotland and set on the banks of the river Clyde, Glasgow is 46mi/74km from Edinburgh and 417mi/671km from London. The city is less than an hour's drive from some of the most beautiful scenery in Europe: the indented, rocky Atlantic coastline to the west, the spectacular scenery of the Highlands to the north and the central lowlands to the east. The minor relief features around the city at Dumbarton, Stirling and Edinburgh are evidence of volcanic activity.

Ashton Lane, in the heart of Glasgow's West End

S. Hughes/MICHELIN

Layout

Early Glasgow consisted of a single main street leading from the Cathedral to the Clyde (now the High St). By the late 18C, new suburbs were opening out to the west areas favoured by rich merchants seeking to escape the squalid confines of the old medieval closes. The West End is home to Glasgow University while the City Centre offers the best collection of shops in Britain outside London. Evidence of the city's resolutely modern outlook can be found in recent eye-catching additions to the Glasgow skyline (The Armadillo, Glasgow Science Centre) or the banks of the Clyde.

■ History
Religious troubles

Although not the capital, Glasgow was part of the British Kingdom of Strathclyde which was bordered to the north by the Picts, to the northwest by the Scots and south by the Angles of Northumbria. St Mungo came to this embattled kingdom in the mid 6C. Proclaimed bishop, he set his wooden church on the banks of the Molendinar Burn. The fish and ring in the

abolishing Episcopacy in Scotland. In February of 1638 the **National Covenant** or Solemn Agreement was drawn up, which pledged the signatories to defend the Crown and true religion. Later in the same year a Covenanter-packed

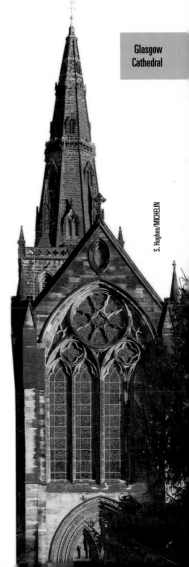

Glasgow Cathedral

S. Hughes/MICHELIN

Glasgow coat of arms refer to a St Mungo legend when he saved an unfaithful wife from the wrath of her royal husband.

A short period of Northumbrian rule in the 7C was followed by incorporation in 1034 into the kingdom of Alba created earlier by the unification of the Pictish and Scottish-held territories. The 12C saw the consecration of the see and the new cathedral of Glasgow. Medieval Glasgow developed around its cathedral and its importance increased with the foundation in 1451 of Scotland's second university and the elevation to archbishopric in 1492.

In the largely Protestant Scotland of the 17C James VI attempted to achieve a situation similar to that in England by re-establishing Episcopacy. This implied royal control of the church through the bishops appointed by the Crown. His son Charles I aroused strong Presbyterian opposition with the forced introduction of the *Scottish Prayer Book*.

Glasgow was the scene of the General Assembly responsible for

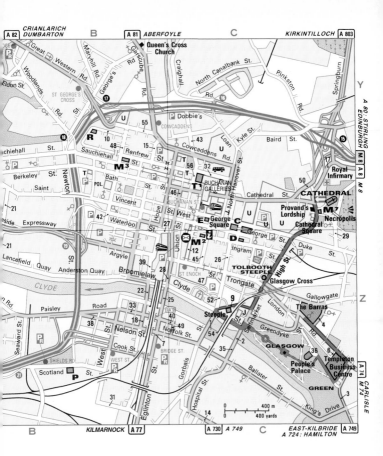

General Assembly at Glasgow abolished Episcopacy, in spite of having been dissolved itself. The Covenanters, under Archibald Campbell 8th Earl of Argyll, took up arms and thus began the First Bishops' War (1639).

The town remained a strong supporter of the Covenanting cause – but the restoration of Episcopacy brought renewed repression for the Covenanters.

In 1643 the **Solemn League and Covenant** united the Covenanters and English parliamentary cause against Charles I. The Covenanters were quick to offer Charles II the throne on his acceptance of the Covenant. Cromwell

Some of Glasgow's magnificent Victorian architectural heritage

marched north defeating the Covenanters' army at **Dunbar** (1650) and Scotland became an occupied country (1651-60) and part of the Commonwealth.

By the 17C trade with the American colonies via Port Glasgow was a feature of Glasgow's commerce. When the obstacles occasioned by the Navigation Acts were eventually overcome by the Union of 1707, this particular trade flourished and early fortunes were made in sugar and rum.

Sugar, tobacco and textiles

Glasgow's growing prosperity in the early 18C depended largely on the tobacco trade (1715-1770s). The outward cargoes of locally manufactured goods were paid for by the return loads of tobacco, which was then re-exported to the continent. The merchants known as **Tobacco Lords** – a restricted group – played an important role in Glasgow's economic and social life. With their traditional outfits of scarlet cloaks and black suits they provided a colourful scene on the plainstones, their exclusive trading patch in front of the Tontine Hotel at Glasgow Cross.

Today's street names, Jamaica, Virginia, Glassford, Dunlop, Miller and Buchan are reminders of this flourishing activity and its merchant families. The American War of Independence caused the eventual decline in the tobacco trade but many of the merchants had invested their accumulated wealth in other emergent industries (banking, textiles, coal mining and iron manufacturing).

Second City of the Empire

Cotton manufacturing in particular was responsible for a large increase in the city's population. This trend continued with the impetus of the Industrial Revolution which brought in its wake the centralisation of heavy industries (coal, iron, and steel) in the Glasgow area. Improved communications – building of the Forth-Clyde and Monkland Canals, arrival of the railways and deepening of the Clyde which was made navigable up to Broomielaw – also played an important role in expansion.

Once Glasgow had become established as an area

of heavy industry, the emphasis moved to shipbuilding with the development of iron ships and screw propulsion. Some of the world's greatest liners were Clyde-built. The prosperity engendered by the Industrial Revolution gave the city its solidly prosperous Victorian face, when it was the workshop of the Empire and came second only to London. This title was lost to Birmingham in 1951.

New era of Scottish democracy

The decline of Scottish industry in the 1930s led to frostier relations between Scotland and the central Government, although the Scots had their own legal and education systems. The economic decline of the last decades and discontent about the lack of adequate benefits from North Sea Oil fostered nationalist feelings. The remoteness of central government, the imposition of the poll tax and local government reorganisation were all contentious issues. As direct election of representatives to the European Parliament had given Scotland renewed confidence in its ability to control its own affairs, the 1997 referendum was a resounding vote for devolution. Scotland greeted the opening of the Scottish Parliament with pride some 290 years after the last parliament was dissolved. The new body opened in Edinburgh in 1999 and has 120 members; the Executive consists of a First Minister and a team of ministers and law officers. The Parliament has responsibility over wide areas of Scottish affairs and has tax-raising powers. Among areas which remain under Westminster control are the constitution, foreign policy, defence and national security, border controls, economic policy, social security, transport safety and employment legislation.

■ Culture
Art

Commercial prosperity begat a new generation of businessmen interested in art, some making bequests (Stephen Mitchell, the tobacco manufacturer) and others (McLellan, Burrell, Sir William Maxwell Stirling) collecting, advised by art collectors like Alexander Reid. Out of this cultural activity a movement, sometimes known as **The Glasgow Boys**, emerged in the last quarter of the 19C partly as a protest against the traditions embodied by the Academicians of Edinburgh and the Victorian artistic conventions.

The leading members were **W Y MacGregor** father of the group, **James Guthrie**, **George Henry**, **E A Hornel** and **John Lavery.** The artists sought to achieve realism as an alternative to the prevalent romanticism, sentimentality and staidness. Masterpieces include *Galloway Landscape* (Henry – Kelvingrove), *Carse of Lecropt* (MacGregor – Hunterian), *The Tennis Party* (Lavery – Aberdeen). In many ways the group was the equivalent of the contemporary Hague and Barbizon schools.

The **Scottish Colourists** (J D Fergusson, F Caddell, S J Peploe, L Hunter) were the next important group to emerge from Glasgow in the early 20C. Their canvases are striking with the strong lines and vibrant colours reminiscent of Post Impressionism and Fauvism: *Bathers, Le Voile Persan, Les Eus* (Fergusson), *The Red Chair* (Caddell), *The Brown Crock, Iona, Tulips and Cup* (Peploe).

This ferment of artistic activity nurtured the development of an **Art Nouveau** movement in the 1890s. The most brilliant exponent was the architect and decorator **Charles Rennie Mackintosh** (1868-1928) who, along with H McNair and the Macdon-

Hampden Park

ald sisters, was responsible for a rebirth in fine and applied arts. Mackintosh revived the Scottish vernacular tradition in his design for the Glasgow School of Art and followed this early design in the Art Nouveau style with Hill House in Helensburgh *(see The CLYDE ESTUARY)*, a work which, even today, some 80 years later still seems modern.

The Glasgow School of Art nurtured many outstanding artists: R Colquhoun (1914-62) – *The Dubliners, Figures in a Farmyard* showing the influence of Cubism – and R MacBryde (1913-66) – *The Backgammon Player, Fish on a Pedestal Table* (original combination of unusual objects).

The **New Image** group from Glasgow is blazing a trail on the contemporary scene. The influence of Fernand Léger and the Mexican muralists is evident in the graphic emphasis of the human figure and the raw vigour of the large compositions by Ken **Currie** (b 1960) – *The Glasgow Triptych* mural. Social realism is also tackled with poetic vision by Peter Howson (b 1958). The works of Adrian Wiszniewski (b 1958) show great imaginative fantasy while Stephen Campbell (b 1953) poses conundrums in natural philosophy with emphasis on gesture and metamorphosis. Stephen **Conroy** (b 1964) who seems to distance himself from human life is famous for his strangely typecast characters (clubmen, actors, singers, businessmen) depicted with great flair and craftsmanship.

Cultural centre, second to none

Glasgow provides a home for **Scottish Opera** and **Scottish Ballet** in a lavishly refurbished Theatre Royal (1975) and a rehearsal and recording base for the

S. Hughes/MICHELIN

Detail, the Italian Centre

Scottish National Orchestra in the SNO centre, Henry Wood Hall. **Glasgow's Mayfest**, founded in 1983, offers a wide range of classical music and attracts much international interest. In 1990, Glasgow was nominated Cultural Capital of Europe, provoking the regeneration of large parts of the city, which had been left derelict by the decline of large-scale heavy industry.

The imposing **Royal Concert Hall** at the north end of Buchanan St provides additional facilities for cultural events. The refurbished McLellan Gallery and the Third Eye Centre (230 and 350 Sauchiehall St respectively) are venues for temporary exhibitions. In 1999 the city was celebrated as the UK City of Architecture and Design as part of an Arts Council Arts 2000 Initiative.

The town also hosts an annual **International Folk Festival**.

■ Science

Scottish scientists have made great contributions to the advancement of science in the fields of medicine, physics, geology, botany, mathematics and engineering. Glasgow universities are at the forefront of advanced scientific research.

Innovation

In the 18C the brothers John and William **Hunter** were leaders in the fields of anatomy and obstetrics. **Sir Joseph Lister**'s (1827-1912) pioneering use of antiseptics was a major success. The physicist William Thomson, **Lord Kelvin** (1824-1907) held a chair at the University of Glasgow and initiated much original research and formulated the second law of thermodynamics. Chloroform was first used as an anaesthetic in 1847 by Sir James Simpson (1811-70). Sir William Hooker (1785-1865), a distinguished English botanist and

the first director of Kew Gardens, worked at Glasgow University and collected specimens in Scotland (1806).

Technical progress

The engineer Henry Bell (1767-1830) designed the first steam-powered boat to ferry passengers on the Clyde. The lighthouses (Bell, Mull) built by Robert Stevenson (1772-1850) are dotted along the coast. Two famous names in the civil engineering world are **Thomas Telford** (1757-1834) and **John Rennie** (1761-1821) who built bridges, roads, canals, docks and harbours. The invention of the steam engine by **James Watt** (1736-1819) revolutionised industrial practices. He was also involved in the building of the Crinan and Caledonian canals. John MacAdam who was born in Ayr in 1756 invented the hard-wearing road surface (small stones compacted in layers) which bears his name.

The world of modern communications is greatly indebted to **Alexander Graham Bell** (1847-1922), the inventor of the telephone. This man of genius also did pioneering work in the medical and aeronautical fields. Another famous name is **John Logie Baird** (1888-1946) who invented television.

■ Overseas ventures

Exploration

The adventurous nature of many Scottish explorers has led to the discovery of unknown territories. The dark continent of Africa lured **Mungo Park** (1771-1806), who ex- plored West Africa and attempted to trace the course of the River Niger. **David Livingstone** (1813-73), a doctor and missionary who campaigned against the slave trade, was the first to cross the African mainland from east to west and discovered the Victoria Falls and Lake Nyasa (now Lake Malawi).

Other famous names include Sir John Ross (1777-1856), the Arctic explorer, and Alexander Mackenzie (1755-1820), a native of Lewis in the Hebrides, who set off for Canada *(see Michelin Green Guide Canada)*. John McDouall Stuart (1815-66) journeyed to Australia and explored the Australian desert.

Scottish Exhibition and Conference Centre (SECC)

New World Connections

Following the Highland Clearances *(see below)*, new horizons for emigrants from Scotland opened up in the New World after the signing of the Treaty of Paris (1773) which ended the Anglo-French War. The province of Nova Scotia in Canada was settled by Highlanders *(see Michelin Green Guide Canada)*. The Scots soon proved their spirit of enterprise; they founded the North West Company (1773) and set up trading posts in competition with the Hudson Bay Company. Among the Scots entrepreneurs were **Alexander Mackenzie**, the first man to cross the North American continent by land (1783), and James McGill (1774-1813) who founded the English-speaking McGill University. Others made their name in Virginia: John Carlyle was a friend of George Washington and a founding trustee of the town of Alexandria *(see Michelin*

Highland Clearances

Following the 1715 and 1745 Jacobite risings, an attempt was made to quell the rebellious Highlanders: the estates of the turbulent clan chiefs were forfeited to the Crown and sold to non-Highland owners. Clansmen who had previously settled their tribute by a period of military service in the chief's army were charged high rents which they could ill afford. Some chiefs also exacted cash rents or sold off their land to raise funds in order to enjoy the pleasures of London life. During the Napoleonic blockade of England with the ensuing shortages of food and imported wool, farming land in the Highlands was given over to sheep breeding mainly by English and Lowland Scot landowners.

The Highlanders were forcibly evicted, their homes burned and their cattle slaughtered. This resulted from the late 18C to mid 19C in large-scale clearance of the Highlands with the backing of the Government, which supplied sheriffs and troops, and the Kirk, which appointed as ministers Lowland Scots who were alien to the Highland way of life. Thousands of dispossessed clansmen emigrated to Canada and Australia and some moved to Glasgow. A small number, however, clung to coastal areas or moved to the Hebrides where they attempted to scratch a meagre living.

Green Guide Washington DC); William Ramsay was also a prosperous merchant in the town. Trade (fur, tobacco, sugar, cotton) with the New World brought prosperity to the Scottish merchants.

Many Scotsmen blazed a trail in the New World. **John Paul Jones** *(see Index)* became an honoured admiral in the American Navy. One of the signatories of the American Declaration of Independence was the Reverend John Witherspoon who was born (1723) in Gifford in Lothian and was the first president of the institution which is now Princeton University. The naturalist John Muir founded the American National Parks. **Alexander Graham Bell** *(see Index)* pursued his distinguished career in Ontario and Nova Scotia. The philanthropist and steel magnate **Andrew Carnegie** made his fortune in America but extended great generosity to his native land.

■ Scottish Specialities

Scottish cooking is characterised by the excellence and quality of the natural products from river, moor, sea and farm.

Soups

These number **Cock-a-Leekie** using fowl, cut leeks and prunes; **Scots** or **Barley Broth**, a vegetable and barley soup; **Game Soup;** Partan Bree a crab soup and **Cullen Skink** made with smoked haddock.

Fish

Of the many varieties of fish, pride of place goes to the **salmon**, be it farmed or wild, from the famous fisheries of the Tay, Spey or Tweed. Served fresh or smoked, it is a luxury dish. **Trout** and **salmon-trout** with their delicately pink flesh are equally appreciated. Breakfast menus often feature the **Arbroath Smokie** – a small salted and smoked haddock; the **Finnan Haddie**, a salted haddock dried on the beach prior to smoking over a peat fire; and the **kipper** a split, salted and smoked herring.

Meat

With such first class beef cattle as the Aberdeen Angus and Galloway and home-bred sheep, it is hardly surprising that the quality of Scotch **beef** and **mutton** is unsurpassed. **Haggis** is the national dish.

Desserts

Succulent **soft fruits** (strawberries, raspberries and blackcurrants) ripened slowly in mild sunshine make an excellent sweet. Other creamsweets like **Cranachan** often incorporate one of the soft fruits. **Atholl Brose** is a secret mixture of honey, oatmeal, malt whisky and cream.

Preserves

Heather honey or Scottish-made jam and marmalade make ideal presents.

■ Whisky –
The water of life

Today the word whisky conjures up a seemingly endless variety on the shelves of supermarkets (whisky, whiskey, bourbon...) while Scotch Whisky is synonymous with a quality product, which possesses an unrivalled international reputation.

The highly competitive whisky industry is Scotland's biggest export earner (over £900 million a year) and one of the government's main sources of revenue (foreign earnings and excise taxes and duty).

A troubled past – Undoubtedly among the earliest distillers of whisky, the Scots have played a major part in the perfection of this art. In the 15C monks were distilling a spirit and soon after it became an everyday domestic occupation. The Union of 1707 brought exorbitant taxation, including the 1713 malt tax. Distilling went underground and smuggling became a way of life. From the illicit stills on the hillsides, the spirit was transported along a smugglers' trail from Speyside to Perth over 140mi/225km of hill country. Excisemen became the scourge of the Highlands. A succession of new laws in the early 19C did nothing to halt illicit distilling until the 1824 Act. The latter sanctioned distillation on payment of a licence fee and duty per gallon produced. Many distilleries were founded after this date including Glenlivet 1824, Fettercairn 1824, and Talisker 1830. Whisky production developed rapidly in the 1880s as the replacement spirit for gin and brandy, which was highly taxed and becoming increasingly scarce owing to the failure of the vine crop. Blending produced a more palatable drink which rapidly achieved universal success. Although blended whiskies still dominate

Malt whisky

The subtle flavours of pure malt whisky distilled according to age-old methods are greatly prized by connoisseurs throughout the world. The distilleries on Speyside (Cardhu, Glenfarclas, Strathisla, Glen Grant, Glenfiddich, Tamnavulin, The Glenlivet and Dallas Dhu) enjoy a prestigious reputation.

Islay in the Hebrides produces distinctive smoky, peaty malts (Laphroaig, Bowmore, Bunnahabhain). There are also many lesser-known malt whisky distilleries close to Glasgow which welcome visitors.

the market, the subtler and finer qualities of a single malt are gaining recognition.

Malt whisky – The original spirit was a malt or straight unblended product of a single malt whisky. What makes a good whisky? The quality and subtle differences in character depends essentially on a combination of certain factors: barley not always home grown, water filtered through peat or over granite, equipment such as the shape of the still and the experience and skill of the stillmen. The 116 single malts are classified into Highland, Lowland or Islay.

Blended whisky – Grain whisky is made from a malted barley and other cereals. The blends are a mixture of a lighter grain with a malt in secret proportions. Blended varieties are subdivided into two categories: de luxe and standard.

Whisky making – The germination of barley steeped in water turns the starch into sugar. The grain is then kiln-dried over a peat fire. Mashing comprises the mixing of the crushed and dried barley with warm water. The remaining barley husks or draff is used as cattle fodder. Yeast is added to the sugary suspension (wort) in huge vats to convert the sugar into alcohol and carbon dioxide. The wash passes into vast copper pot stills. Two distillations are common to produce the high proof distillate before it is matured in oak barrels in Scotland for a minimum of three years. ■

World Pipe Band Championships

MAIN SIGHTS

CENTRAL GLASGOW

See city plan

George **Square** – Today the heart of Glasgow, the busy square is lined by imposing 19C buildings. Development of the square and adjoining streets began in 1782 and by the beginning of the 19C it had become the city's hotel centre. The initial steps towards a change in character came with the building of the Merchants' House closely followed by the General Post Office and City Chambers.

On the north side is the only hotel to remain (now the Copthorne). The **Merchants' House** (f 1869)

S. Hughes/MICHELIN

George Square

on the west side, and today the home of the Glasgow Chamber of Commerce, is denoted by the Ship of Trade aloft, a replica of the one in Bridgegate. On the south are the post office buildings. Occupying all the east side are the **City Chambers★**, another of Glasgow's magnificent Victorian buildings, a heritage from the time when Glasgow was the second city of the Empire. Inside, grandeur and opulence reign supreme, particularly in the loggia, council and banqueting halls.

Sir Walter Scott on the central column dominates a series of famous men: (clockwise) Peel, Gladstone, Lord Clyde, John Moore, Watt...

Hutchesons' Hall – *NTS Visitor Centre*. The "hospital" of the original endowment of 1639 for 11 old men and 12 orphan boys was demolished when Hutcheson Street was opened up. The replacement institutional headquarters (1802-05) were designed by David Hamilton to provide the focal point for one of the new thoroughfares of the Merchant City. Statues of the two founding Hutcheson brothers were removed from the original building to occupy niches on the main frontage. Two of Glasgow's best-known public schools originate from the early endowment. The refurbished Hutchesons' Hall is now the Glasgow offices and shop of the National Trust for Scotland.

Gallery of Modern Art★ – Glasgow's new and controversial collection of contemporary art is housed in what in the late 18C was the city's most splendid mansion. Built for the tobacco lord William Cunninghame, the great neo-Classical structure boasts a massive Corinthian portico and a magnificent main hall with a barrel-vault ceiling. At the very heart of the commercial city, it served for more than a century as the Royal Exchange, the focal point of Glasgow's business life, then as a library. In the mid 1990s it underwent extensive conversion and now comprises four galleries: Earth *(main hall)*, Fire *(basement)*, Water *(first floor)* and Air *(roof space)*, together with workshops and interactive computer stations. The collection, though new, is already quite extensive, is expanding, and has become a major attraction, commanding attention not least because of the colourful reflective motifs inserted in the portico's pediment. International as well as Scottish artists are represented, the principal criterion for inclusion being art that people can "experience and enjoy".

The range of works selected (sculpture, graphic works, photographs, mobiles and installations as well as paintings) has caused controversy within the art world, not least because of the inclusion of pictures by "popular" painters like

Beryl Cook (*Karaoke*, 1992). But there are plenty of "mainstream" living British artists represented too, like Sir Anthony Caro (*Table Piece Z85 "Tiptoe"* 1982), Ian Hamilton Finlay (*Star/Steer* 1966), Andy Goldsworthy (*Overcast Cold/Upturned Leaves... Sidobre, 4 June 1989*), David Hockney (*Illustration from "Fourteen Poems by C P Cavafy"* 1966) and Bridget Riley (*Arrest III* 1965).

Contributions from abroad include works by the Hungarian pioneer of Op Art, Victor Vasarely, Peter Angermann (*Baggersee* 1988), the Tinguely-influenced maker of mechanical marvels, Eduard Bersud-sky (*The Great Idea, Karl Marx*), and Niki de Saint-Phalle (*Autel du Chat Mort* 1962), and there are intriguing Australian Aboriginal paintings by Robert Campbell Jr (*Who Said You Could Fish Here* 1988) and Paddy Japaljarri Sims (*The Night Sky Dreaming* 1993).

The Lighthouse – *Mitchell Lane*. The former offices of The Glasgow Herald designed by C R Mackintosh have been imaginatively converted into a Centre for Architecture and Design with exhibition galleries, conference hall and educational facilities. It hosts temporary exhibitions.

Glasgow School of Art* – Charles Rennie Mackintosh designed this major landmark in the history of European architecture when he was only 28. The building was completed in two stages, 1897-99 and 1907-09 and nearly 100 years later it remains highly functional while also housing one of the largest collections of Mackintosh furniture, designs and paintings. Of particular interest is the Library, an architectural *tour de force* with its three-storey high windows and suspended ceiling and Mackintosh's most original and celebrated interior. Visitors can also see his decorative stained glass, metalwork, light fittings etc in the Board Room, Director's Room and the Furniture Gallery, which contains furniture designed for the School, Miss Cranston's Tea Rooms and "Windyhill".

The Tenement House – This tenement flat consists of two rooms, kitchen and bathroom and evokes tenement life in the 19C. The original fittings include the box-beds, gas lamps and coal-fired ranges with coal bin. The housing demands of Glasgow's ever increasing population were met by building tenements. They ranged from the humble single-end to the grander and highly desirable residences of the West End. Community life centred on the close and back court. ■

Gallery of Modern Art

GLASGOW CATHEDRAL***

See city plan

This imposing Gothic building today stands hemmed in by the Royal Infirmary with the Necropolis behind. The best **view**★ of the cathedral as a whole is from John Knox's stance high up in the Necropolis where the verticality of the composition is best appreciated. This is the fourth church on the site beside the Molendinar Burn, where **St Mungo** built his original wooden church in the 7C. The main part of the cathedral was built in the 13C and 14C with construction progressing from the east end to the nave, and it was the 15C before the building took on its final appearance with the reconstruction of the chapter house and addition of the Blacader Aisle, central tower and stone spire, and the now demolished west front towers. Unusual features of the plan are the non-projecting transepts and two-storeyed east end.

Interior – There is a satisfying impression of unity, although building spanned a period of 300 years. Here the pointed arch reigns supreme.

Nave – It is stylistically later than the choir and the elevation with its richly moulded and pointed arches, ever more numerous at each level, rises to the timber roof. The 15C stone screen or pulpitum, unique in Scotland, marks the change in level from nave to choir. The figures at the top of the screen depict the seven deadly sins; the human figures on the front of the altar platforms may represent 11 disciples.

Choir – The choir and the lower church, both dating from the mid 13C, are of the finest First Pointed style. The great beauty derives from a combination of harmonious elevations and finely worked details. Note in particular the varied and vigorously carved foliate capitals and corbels and gaily tinctured bosses of the ambulatory vaulting, behind the high altar. The triple lancets of the clerestory are echoed in the design of the east window which depicts the Four Evangelists. Four chapels open out of the ambulatory beyond. From the northernmost chapel a door leads through to the upper chapter room, reconstructed in the 15C. It was there that the medieval university held its classes.

Lower Church – *Access via stairs to north of the pulpitum.* Here is another Gothic glory where light and shade play effectively amidst a multitude of piers and pointed arches. This lower area was conceived to enshrine the **tomb of St Mungo**, Glasgow's patron saint. A cordoned-off area marks the site. The central panel of the St Kentigern Tapestry (1979) represents the Church and combines the symbols of St Mungo. On the south panel are the ring and salmon of the St Mungo legend. The tapestry was woven by the Edinburgh Dovecot Studios to the designs of Robert Stewart. The Chapel of the Blessed Virgin is the area immediately to the east, distinguished by its elaborate net vaulting with intricately carved bosses.

The mid-13C lower chapter room was remodelled at the time of Bishop William Lauder (1408-25). The bishop's arms figure on the canopy. The 15C ribbed vaulting sports heraldic roof bosses including the arms of James I.

Blacader Aisle – Projecting from the south transept, this last addition to the church was designed as a two-storey extension by Glasgow's first Archbishop, Robert Blacader. Only the existing or lower part was finished. The Late Gothic style with its fully developed ribbed vaulting gives an effect of richness. Look for the carved boss (facing the entrance) recalling the legend of the hermit Fergus, who was found near to death by St Mungo. The next day the body was placed on a cart yoked to two bulls with the intention of burying the hermit where they stopped. Some say this chapel marks the site. ∎

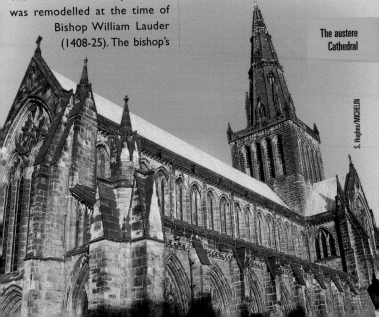

The austere Cathedral

S. Hughes/MICHELIN

MEDIEVAL GLASGOW

See city plan

■ Cathedral Square to Glasgow Green

The main road from the cathedral to the bridgehead followed this route to Glasgow Cross then branched to the right via Bridgegate.

St Mungo Museum of Religious Life and Art – 2 Castle Street. Since its opening in 1993 this museum has sparked controversy with its collections of religious artefacts grouped in three galleries: **Religious Art** contains the museum's best-known painting, Dali's *St John of the Cross*, as well as a 19C bronze Shiva and an Islamic prayer rug; **Religious Life** deals with the myriad ways in which religion is part of everyday life, while **Religion in Scotland** surveys the variety of faiths practised in the country over the last 5 000 years. A fourth gallery houses temporary exhibitions and there is an authentic Japanese Zen garden.

Cathedral Square – Prior to the Reformation this was the very heart of the ecclesiastical city. Cathedral, Bishop's Castle and canons' manses overlooked this focal point. The Bishop's Castle (a stone in the Royal Infirmary forecourt marks the site) was destroyed to

S. Hughes/MICHELIN

make way for the Adam brothers' 1792 Royal Infirmary building. The present **Royal Infirmary** is a 20C replacement. It was in a ward of the original one that **Sir Joseph Lister** (1827-1912) pioneered the use of carbolic acid as an antiseptic in the treatment of wounds.

The statues in the square include one of the missionary explorer David Livingstone *(see Index)* and an equestrian statue of King William of Orange.

Necropolis – Behind the cathedral on the far bank of the Molendinar Burn is the formal burial garden dating from 1833. Pathways bordered by elaborate tombs lead up to the highest point commanded by John Knox atop his column. There is a good **view*** of the cathedral and Glasgow away to the southwest.

Provand's Lordship – Provand's Lordship, a former prebendal manse dating from 1471, and the cathedral are the only survivors of the medieval town. The two lower floors are furnished with 16C–20C pieces.

High Street – A plaque on the disused goods yard opposite College Street marks the site of Old College from 1632 to 1870 and the original Hunterian Museum prior to their transfer to Gilmorehill. At 215 High Street, the former British Linen Bank building is still crowned by the figure of Pallas, goddess of wisdom and weaving. The stained glass above the door portrays a flax boat.

The Necropolis

Glasgow Cross – Until Victorian times the Cross at the junction of High Street, Saltmarket, Gallowgate and Trongate was the heart of Glasgow. Defoe much admired the Cross set as it was at the centre of a prosperous commercial area known as the "Golden Acre". The **Tolbooth Steeple***, in the middle of the street, is a striking reminder of this former elegance. The seven-storey tower was originally adjoined by the elegant tolbooth and then the Tontine Hotel. The **mercat cross** nearby is a 1929 replica.

Bridgegate – This now rather dismal street was once a fashionable main thoroughfare to the city's first stone bridge built in 1345. The **steeple**, rising out of derelict warehouses is all that remains of the 1659 Merchants Hall (demolished 1818), the business and social meeting place for Glasgow's merchants. The steeple rising in tiers to a height of 164ft/50m served as a lookout for cargoes coming up the Clyde. The Ship of Trade in full sail symbolises the origins of Glasgow's trade. A new Merchants' House was built in 1877 in George Square (*see CENTRAL GLASGOW*).

The Saltmarket took over as the main thoroughfare in the 19C.

Glasgow Green – On the north bank of the Clyde this park is one of Glasgow's most historic sites. Successively

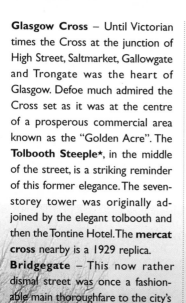

or simultaneously it was a place of common grazing, bleaching, public hangings, military reviews and parades, merry-making at Glasgow Fair and above all of public meetings and free speech. Alternating between fashionable and disreputable, it has always been most fiercely defended against encroachment and today lies within the GEAR (Glasgow Eastern Area Renewal Scheme) revitalisation programme. Monuments on the Green include the now sadly abandoned Doulton Fountain – a remarkable piece of pottery figuring Queen Victoria – one to Nelson and the nearby stone commemorating the spot where James Watt, while out on a Sunday walk, worked out his improvement to the steam engine.

People's Palace – *Enter by Morris Place.* The People's Palace museum and winter gardens were opened in 1898 as a cultural centre for the east end. It is now a local and social history museum, and the exhibits recount the story of Glasgow from earliest times to the present. There is an exotic plant display in the winter gardens.

Templeton Business Centre – This highly unusual, colourful and richly decorated Doge's Palace, which was built in 1889, originally housed a carpet factory.

The Barras – A lively weekend market. An assortment of goods at bargain prices, colourful characters and street entertainment are some of the attractions of a visit to the Barras. Refurbishment and pedestrian precincts have followed in the wake of a renewal programme. ■

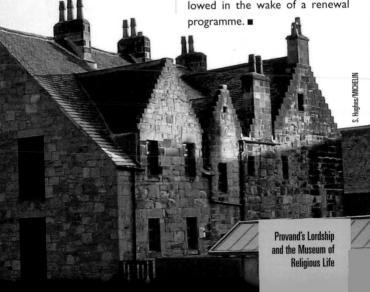

S. Hughes/MICHELIN

Provand's Lordship and the Museum of Religious Life

THE WEST END***

See plan below

■ Glasgow University

Bishop William Turnbull founded the university in 1451 and the first classes were held in the cathedral. The early university was greatly dependent on the church and the bishops and archbishops of Glasgow held the office of Chancellor until 1642. The university then acquired properties in the High Street which were used until 1632 when the **Old College**, a handsome building arranged around a double quadrangle, was built. The High Street premises were abandoned and destroyed in 1870 when the university moved to the present site on the estate of Gilmorehill in the west end of the city.

The consequent imposing edifice remains the focal point of a complex of new (Adam Smith, Boyd Orr and Hetherington Buildings, Hunterian Art Gallery and Library) and refurbished buildings throughout the local streets. Today eight faculties (Arts, Divinity, Engineering, Law, Medicine, Science, Social and Veterinary Medicine) welcome over 13 000 students.

Gilmorehill Building – This massive Gothic Revival building, the oldest of the university's present buildings, was designed by George Gilbert Scott. The project was not completed owing to a lack of funds, and it was Scott's son, John Oldrid, who completed the design with Bute Hall (1882) and the tower (1887). The main façade overlooks Kelvingrove Park. In Professors' Square at the west end of the main building is the **Lion and Unicorn Staircase** from the Old College, as are the staircase and Pearce Lodge facing University Avenue.

The **Visitor Centre** caters for the University's 80 000 annual visitors with informative displays, interactive computers and a camera obscura showing the panorama from the building's tall tower.

Hunterian Museum – *Main building, East Quadrangle, First Floor; enter from University Avenue side.* William Hunter (1718-83), successful medical practitioner, anatomist and pioneer obstetrician, was also a great collector, investing in coins, manuscripts, paintings, minerals, and ethnographical, anatomical and zoological specimens. Hunter bequeathed all to the university and in 1807 the Hunterian Museum was opened. His brother John's collection formed the nucleus of a second Hunterian Museum, now in the Royal College of Surgeons, London. Today William's treasured items are divided between the museum and the art gallery.

Museum – The first gallery presents a historical introduction to the university and its many famous sons. The Hunter **coin and medal collection***, once said to be second only to the French Royal Collection is exhibited in a purpose-built gallery. A chronological presentation from a collection of over 30 000 items traces the development of coinage from ancient times to the present. The earliest Scottish coinage appeared in 1136 and by the late 12C-early 13C there were no fewer than 16 mints, the greatest number ever. No coins have been minted in Scotland since the closure of the

Edinburgh Mint in the 18C following the Treaty of Union. Note the rare example of Scotland's first gold coin issued c 1357 by David II and one of James V's bonnet pieces using Scottish gold. The endpiece of the collection is the 1984 pound coin with the Scottish design on the reverse. Exhibits in the main hall, beyond, cover material from Captain Cook's voyages, a pleasant display on the Romans in Scotland, early civilisations and British prehistory. The upper gallery is devoted to geology and ar-

S. Hughes/MICHELIN

The Gothic
Gilmorehill Tower
at Glasgow University

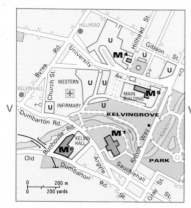

cheology. Do not miss recent finds, the Bearsden Shark and the only evidence of a Scottish dinosaur.

Hunterian Art Gallery★★ (M2) – The 1980 building provides a permanent home for the university's art collection which is particularly noted for the Whistler works, 19C and 20C Scottish art and the Mackintosh wing. Outstanding among the Old Masters are Rembrandt's *The Entombment* (1) and Rubens' *Head of an Old Man* (1). Alongside canvases by the portraitists Raeburn *(Mrs Hay of Spot,* 2), Ramsay (the founder *William Hunter,* 2), Romney and Reynolds, are several by Stubbs and Chardin. The **Whistler Collection★★★ (4, 5** and **6)** is an important holding covering most periods of the career of **James McNeill Whistler** (1834-1903). Examples of portraiture include the strik-

ing group of full-lengths *(Pink and Silver – The Pretty Scamp; Red and Black – The Fan* and *Pink and Gold – The Tulip;* all in 4). A master in the art of etching, the French, Thames and Venetian sets demonstrate his stylistic development.

The remaining galleries present 19C and 20C Scottish art together with some French Impressionists. Breaking away from the conventions of Victorian art, William **McTaggart** (1835-1910) developed his own bold style with vigorous brushwork and a sensitive approach to light *(The Sound of Jura, The Fishers' Landing* 3). He was a precursor of the late-19C group, the **Glasgow Boys**, which originated as a response to the staidness of the Edinburgh art establishment and whose common denominator was realism. Acknowledged father of the group was W McGregor *(Carse of Lecropt)*; other members included Hornel *(Gathering Primroses, Japanese figures)*, Guthrie *(The Gypsy Fires)*, Henry, Walton and Lavery **(7, 10)**.

Pringle's townscapes *(Tollcross* 10) in delicate pastel tones herald the **Scottish Colourists (8)**: *Les Eus, Le Voile Persan* by Fergusson, *Iona, Tulips and Cup* by Peploe, *The Red Chair* by Caddell and works by Hunter. The modern section includes an atmospheric canvas by Joan Eardley *(Salmon Nets and the Sea* 1960), Philipson's *Never Mind* (1965) and Davie's *Sea Devil's Watch Tower* (1960).

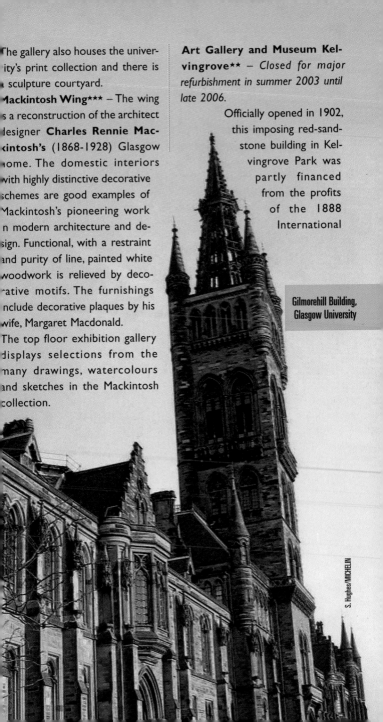

The gallery also houses the university's print collection and there is a sculpture courtyard.

Mackintosh Wing★★★ – The wing is a reconstruction of the architect designer **Charles Rennie Mackintosh's** (1868-1928) Glasgow home. The domestic interiors with highly distinctive decorative schemes are good examples of Mackintosh's pioneering work in modern architecture and design. Functional, with a restraint and purity of line, painted white woodwork is relieved by decorative motifs. The furnishings include decorative plaques by his wife, Margaret Macdonald.

The top floor exhibition gallery displays selections from the many drawings, watercolours and sketches in the Mackintosh collection.

Art Gallery and Museum Kelvingrove★★ – *Closed for major refurbishment in summer 2003 until late 2006.*

Officially opened in 1902, this imposing red-sandstone building in Kelvingrove Park was partly financed from the profits of the 1888 International

Gilmorehill Building,
Glasgow University

S. Hughes/MICHELIN

Exhibition on the same site. The nucleus of the permanent collection was formed by the McLellan Bequest (1854) and ever since, prominent citizens and captains of industry such as Graham-Gilbert, James Donald and William McInnes have generously continued to bequeath their art treasures, making this one of the outstanding civic collections. The visitor should make a particular effort to visit the first floor galleries.

Ground floor – The sections of particular interest on this floor are the Scottish Natural History display (east court), the attractively presented European arms and armour (west court) and Scottish weapons, as well as Neolithic, Bronze, Iron Age and Roman material. The Glasgow Style gallery displays the work of Charles Rennie Mackintosh and his Glasgow contemporaries.

First floor – The upper galleries are devoted to fine and decorative arts particularly glass, silver, ceramics and jewellery, and British and European paintings.

ITALIAN AND SPANISH – Giorgione's *The Adulteress brough before Christ* is accompanied b the fragment *Head of a Man. Th Baptism in the Jordan* is a goo example of Salvator Rosa's work There are also fine works b Filippino Lippi, Domenichino an Guardi. The moving *St Peter Re pentant* is by Ribera.

DUTCH AND FLEMISH – The gal lery has a particularly good hold ing of 17C paintings. Major work include Jacob Jordaens' colourfu *The Fruit Seller*, Van Orley's movin *Virgin and Child* and a combine composition by Rubens an Bruegel the Elder, *Nature Adorne by the Graces*. Rembrandt is rep resented by *A Man in Armour* an the earlier still-life *The Carcase o an Ox*. Alongside are notable land scapes by Jacob van Ruisdael.

FRENCH – There is a strong emphasis on 19C and early 20C works. Open-air painters of the Barbizon School such as Millet,

Daubigny and Harpignies were the forerunners of the Impressionists. Millet's *Going to Work* is a major canvas of this period. Fantin-Latour is represented by several works including *Chrysanthemums* and Courbet by a major still-life *Flower in a basket*.

Beyond, compare the various Impressionist works by Monet (*Vétheuil*), Pissarro, Renoir and Sisley. The Van Gogh portrait of the famous Glasgow art dealer *Alexander Reid* (1887) was painted when the artist and dealer shared rooms in Paris. Reid was responsible for promoting the Impressionists in Scotland and many of the collection's works came through his hands. The bronze of Reid by Benno Schotz was done a year before the sitter died (1927). Other contemporaries of Van Gogh were Cézanne and Gauguin.

Later movements are represented by Vuillard (*Mother and Child*) and the Nabis, Braque and Picasso, the Cubists, Derain (*Blackfriars*), Matisse and the Fauves.

BRITISH – The regal full-length of *Archibald 3rd Duke of Argyll* and the *Dowager Countess of Stafford* show the range of the 18C portraitist Allan Ramsay. Works by Raeburn (*Mr and Mrs Campbell* and the very Scottish *Mrs Anne Campbell of Park*) hang alongside those by Reynolds and Romney.

David Wilkie and the Faed brothers excelled in historical and domestic scenes while the awesome grandeur of Scottish scenery was well captured by Horatio McCulloch (*Glencoe*).

The Pre-Raphaelites (Burne-Jones, Ford Madox Brown and Rossetti) combine symbolism and a liking for sharp detail.

The works of William McTaggart with free, bold brushwork and feeling for light, break from the traditions of his time. *Dawn at sea – homewards* is an example of that very luminous quality.

The last room is devoted to the Glasgow Boys (*see Introduction: Art*). One of the leading works

Art Gallery and Museum Kelvingrove

is Henry's *A Galloway Landscape*. The Henry-Hornel compositions show a distinctively Japanese flavour. The colourful canvases of the Scottish Colourists who were active in the late 19C-early 20C show the influence of Fauvism: *The Brown Crock* (Peploe), *The Pink Parasol, Montgeron* (Fergusson), *Old Mill Fife, Sails Venice* (Hunter) and *Interior, the Orange Blind* (Cadell). The modern era is represented by Joan Eardley's evocative *A Stormy Sea* and Anne Redpath's *Pinks*.

Museum of Transport★★ – The comprehensive collections cover all forms of transport, excepting aviation. Take plenty of time and be prepared to be side-tracked and delighted by this fascinating collection.

Ground floor

Trams and trolley buses – A raised catwalk allows visitors to inspect the upper decks of the vintage tramcars which were so much part of Glasgow's street scene from 1872 to 1962.

These vehicles are arranged in chronological order and include no 543, the horse-drawn one, no 1 089, the 1926 single-deck car and no 1 392 of the type nicknamed the Cunarder because of its comfort, the last tram ever built in the UK (1952). This extremely popular collection was the nucleus around which the museum was established. The trolley-bus is an example from the fleet which operated in Glasgow from 1949 to 1967.

Railway locomotives – Most of the seven items on display are from the former Scottish railway companies. There is also a fascinating model railway, a spell-binder for all ages.

Glasgow Botanic Gardens

Motor cars – The emphasis is on **cottish-built cars***** with examples from manufacturers such as Argyll, Albion and Arrol-Johnston, who were all well to the fore in the car industry of the early 20C. The great traditions of Scottish car manufacturing are represented here by the 1902 Argyll Light Car, the 1906 Arrol-Johnston TT Model 18, fast and powerful for its time and the Argyll Voiturette. The 1963 Hillman Imp, IMP 1 was the first Scottish-built car after a lapse of 30 years.

Horse-drawn vehicles – The varied examples of horse-drawn vehicles on display include the splendid Mail Coach (c 1840) and the two Romany caravans which are brightly painted with tradional decoration.

Fire vehicles – This section (behind the Scottish cars) covers a range of fire fighting equipment from the earliest used by insurance companies, those powered by steam to the most modern Leyland Firemaster.

Kelvin Street – This shop-lined street evokes life as it was on 1 December 1938. The subway station is a cherished reminder of Glasgow's subway prior to modernisation in the 1970s.

Mezzanine

Bicycles and motor cycles – Follow the development of the bicycle from the replica of MacMillan's 1839 bicycle (on the wall)

through boneshakers, sociables and tricycles to the gleaming lightweight road racers and fun cycles of today.

The motor cycle section has early examples of British-designed machines from the time when British makers dominated the industry (Zenith, BSA, Triumph, AJS, Beardmore-Precision, Norton and Douglas).

The Clyde Room of Ship Models*** – This beautifully presented collection displays the products of the Scottish shipyards through the ages and in particular those of the Clyde. Side by side are perfect models of sailing ships (the fully rigged *Cutty Sark*), Clyde River Steamers (*Comet, Columba* and other well-loved excursion steamers), cross-Channel steamers which were often Denny products, ocean-going passenger liners *(The Queens)*, warships (HMS *Hood*) and yachts including the Czar Alexander II's circular and unsinkable model.

Botanic Gardens – *By B 808.* The gardens are renowned for their collection of orchids, begonias and tree ferns. The Kibble Palace, which houses the tree ferns and plants from temperate areas, is a unique example of a Victorian iron conservatory. The Main Range contains the tropical and economic plants. A Scottish Garden planted with plants endemic to Scotland is being created. ■

THE BURRELL COLLECTION★★★

3mi/5km southwest by M 77 – see city pla
The museum stands in the grounds of Pollok Hous

A visit to the Burrell Collection is a must in order to appreciate the collector for his achievement, the collection for its scope and depth and the imaginative and thoroughly modern building for its accomplished accommodation and enhancement of the treasures.

The collection – It is important to bear in mind that the Collection was amassed by one man, essentially for his own pleasure. Burrell continued buying for the collection even after he had handed it over to public ownership. In about 80 years of collecting, with resources far below those of the millionaire class such as Frick, Hearst and Mellon, Burrell showed taste, insight, discernment and determination in his pursuit and acquisition of the more than 8 000 items. He had strong personal preferences for the medieval glass and tapestries, Chinese ceramics and 19C French paintings. In his latter years he made a determined effort to increase the comprehensiveness of the collection with a view to its becoming public.

The collector – Characteristical this very private man, **Sir Willian Burrell** (1861-1958), maintaine that "the Collection and not th collector is the important thing William joined the family shipow ing firm at the early age of 14 an by 40 he and his brother had mad their fortunes. After the final sa of the fleet during the First Worl War he spent the rest of his li amassing his vast art collectio which he housed in his Glasgo home at 8 Great Western Terrac and then in Hutton Castle. Fro 1911 Burrell kept a full record his activities in 28 school jotte known as the Purchase Book In 1944, at the age of 82 he be queathed his treasures to his n tive city with strict conditions fc housing the collection: "in a rur setting far removed from the a mospheric pollution of urban cc urbations, not less than 16 mile from the Royal Exchange."

The building – In 1983, almc 40 years later and after years indecision, delays, disappointmen propositions and counter-propos tions, the Collection found a pe nanent home and was finally on display to the public. The elegant modern custom-built building of warm red sandstone, light wood and walls of glass in its parkland etting with a woodland backdrop, successfully enhances the varied items of the collection. The result fulfils Burrell's own wishes "as simple as possible" to house the "fine contents".

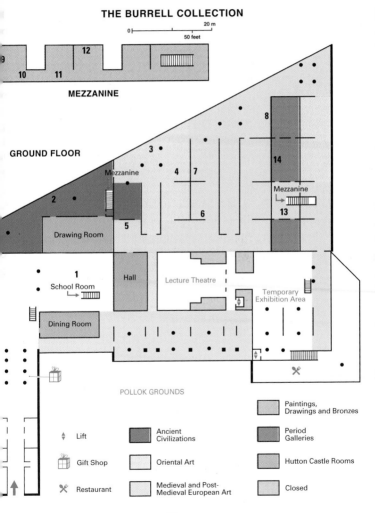

THE BURRELL COLLECTION

■ Tour 1hr 30min

For those with little time to spare, the major works are located on the accompanying plan. As only parts of the collection can be shown at any one time, certain sections may change periodically.

Ancient Civilisations – The 2C AD **Warwick Vase** (1), the centrepiece of the courtyard, is an 18C marble reconstruction incorporating some of the original fragments found at Hadrian's Villa, Tivoli.

The work is a recent Trustees' acquisition. Compare the balance, proportion and naturalism of the Egyptian items (head of Sekhmet-18th dynasty, *shawabti* burial figures, bronze of Osiris), designed for eternity, with the later Greek works often having motifs derived from the Near East.

The skill of the Greek vase painter is displayed in the 4C BC bell krater from Lucania in red-figure earthenware and the lekythos attributed to the Gela Painter (c 6C-5C BC).

The noble porphyry **Head of Zeus or Poseidon** (2), a 4C AD Roman copy of a Greek bronze, shows as much realism as the mosaic cockerel, also Roman, of 1C BC. The Mesopotamian terracotta lion head of the Isin-Larsa period (c 2020-1600 BC) probably belonged to a protective figure in a temple.

Oriental Art – Burrell had a particular fondness for Chinese ceramics, bronzes, jades and this wide-ranging section has items from the 3rd millennium BC to the 19C. The charming earthenware watchdog with its intricate harness and the Boshanlu jar and cover are good examples of the earliest pieces from the Han Dynasty (3C BC-3C AD).

The camel, horse and attendant and tomb figures are 8C Tang Dynasty. These earthenware objects all display green, amber and cream lead glazes.

Set against the woodland backdrop is the serenely seated figure of a **lohan** (3) or disciple of Buddha. Almost life-size, this Ming Dynasty (1366-1644) figure dated 1484 is a masterpiece of enamel biscuit ware. The superbly decorated underglaze red-decoration **ewer (4)** is of the late-14C Ming period. The decorative scheme includes two cartouches filled with a lotus scroll of five flowers, varyingly open and shut. The full range and beauty of the ceramics, bronzes and jades can be appreciated by following the porcelain corridor.

Medieval and Post-Medieval European Art – The tapestry and stained glass sections are the highlights of this department. Admire the group of tapestries, in particular the 15C Tournai **Peasants Hunting Rabbits with Ferrets (5)** so alive with amazing and amusing details, and the 16C *Flight of the Heron*. The decorative themes relate to allegory, mythology and romance. There are also heraldic and purely decorative scenes.

The stained glass bay rewards a close inspection. The 12C fragment from the then Abbey Church of St Denis (near Paris) figures the **Prophet Jeremiah (6)**.

Stained glass is also daringly used in the glass wall south of the building.

The Romanesque bronze, the **Temple Pyx (7)**, shows three sleeping warriors. On the wall above is a delicate alabaster Virgin and Child and opposite stands the Bury Chest. Both are important 14C English works. A Pietà by the workshop of the Rimini Master, a Burgundian altarpiece **(8)** and

an alabaster Virgin and Child are fine examples of 15C European sculpture.

Paintings, Drawings and Bronzes – *Mezzanine*. The early works include Giovanni Bellini's delightful *Virgin and Child* **(9)** with the child dangling a flower by a thread. **Cupid, the Honey Thief (10)** and **The Stag Hunt** are important works by Cranach.

Burrell gathered together a notable holding of 19C French paintings. In Room 16 hang Géricault's striking *Prancing Grey Horse* (11), *The Print Collector* by Daumier, seaside scenes *(The Jetty at Trouville)* by Boudin and Fantin-Latour's *Spring Flowers* and works by the Barbizon School including Corot, Millet and Daubigny. In Room 17 Degas is well represented by examples of his two favourite subjects, dancers and horses. The pastel *Jockeys in the Rain* (12) shows a strong sense of movement. *Women Drinking Beer* and *Roses in a Champagne Glass* illustrate Manet's skilful brushwork. Room 18 is used for special displays from the museum's collection including works by the Hague School (the Maris brothers), Joseph Crawhall (member of the Glasgow Boys), Dürer, Le Nain and Whistler among others.

On the ground floor, the 17C-18C period room presents a selection of portraits : **Portrait of a Gentleman** (Frans Hals, 13) at £14 500 the most expensive item in the original collection, Rembrandt's youthful **Self-Portrait** (14) and Hogarth's *Mrs Ann Lloyd*.

Bronzes (Rodin, Epstein) are displayed in the courtyard and in the southeast gallery on the ground floor.

Hutton Castle Rooms – Burrell stipulated that the Hall, Drawing and Dining rooms from Hutton Castle should be incorporated in the gallery. Arranged around the courtyard they are furnished with fine panelling, tapestries, medieval fireplaces, antique furniture, precious carpets and stained glass. The objets d'art include interesting examples of medieval sculpture.

Pollok House* – *3mi/5km southwest of the city centre by the M 77 – plan below.*

The highlight of this 18C mansion, set in spacious parkland, is a superb collection of paintings acquired by the connoisseur and collector **Sir William Stirling Maxwell** (1818-78). He was a pioneer authority on the Spanish School of painting, and his enlightened acquisitions form a most representative collection, which today is displayed in a setting of elegant and tastefully furnished rooms.

Paintings** – The most memorable pictures in the collection are two superb portraits by El Greco

seeglasgow.com

Pollok House

(Library). Other important pictures include Tristan's *Adoration of the Kings* and Alonso Cano's *Adam and Eve* in the Drawing-Room; the series of etchings *Los Disparates* by Goya in the Dining-Room Corridor; Murillo's *Madonna and Child with St John* in the Billiard Room Corridor.

In addition there are canvases by Sanchez Coello, Spanish Court Painter (Billiard Room), Morales, S del Piombo, Jordaens, Mengs, Kneller, Hogarth, Knox and Nasmyth. Works by William Blake *(Chaucer and the Canterbury Pilgrims)* are displayed in the main corridor.

The Maxwell family portraits hang in the Entrance Hall, a late-19C addition. ∎

EXCURSIONS

THE CLYDE ESTUARY

Argyle and Bute; Renfrewshire and Inverclyde

Michelin Atlas p 54 and 55 or Map 501 – G 15

The Clyde Estuary by boat – During July and August the paddle steamer *Waverley* visits the Firth of Clyde resorts with departures from Glasgow, Helensburgh, Dunoon, Rothesay, Largs, Millport and Ayr. In the 19C a succession of paddle steamers sailed the Clyde taking Glaswegians "doon the water" for the day. *The Waverley*, the last of these famous Clyde paddle steamers, plies her home waters in the high season. The day or half-day cruises are an excellent way of discovering the attractive Clyde estuary and its many resorts. For descriptions of the individual sights see below.

The Clyde Estuary★: north shore to Dunoon via the Cowal Peninsula – *77mil/124km, 2hr excluding visiting times.*

The Waverley

Leave Glasgow by Great Western Road and A 82. Branch off to the left in the direction of Dumbarton and Helensburgh.

The distillery and bonded warehouses on the left are guarded by a flock of geese, after the Roman fashion.

Dumbarton Castle – The castle has a strategic **site*** perched on the basaltic plug, Dumbarton Rock (240ft/73m). The rock was once the capital of the independent Kingdom of Strathclyde (incorporated into Scotland 1034), a royal seat, and then in medieval times a much disputed stronghold. The remaining fortifications are mainly 18C. Steps *(278 from the Governor's House)* lead up to the viewing-table on White Tower summit and then to the Magazine on the second summit *(an additional 81 steps)*. From the former viewpoint there is a vast **panorama** of the Clyde estuary and surrounding area. In 1548 the five-year-old Mary, Queen of Scots left Dumbarton for a new life in France. There, Mary spent the next 14 years, with the children of Henri II and Catherine de'Medici.

Cardross – Population 1 841. It was in the vicinity of this village that Robert the Bruce died in 1329.

Hill House, Helensburgh★
– *Upper Colquhoun Street*. On a hillside overlooking the Clyde stands what is considered to be the best example of Mackintosh's domestic architecture. The house was built in 1902-04 as a family home for the Glasgow publisher Walter W Blackie. It was designed as a whole by Mackintosh who lavished the utmost care on the tiniest detail. Everything bears the indelible stamp of his genius. Every space corridor, hall, bed or seating alcove was nobly proportioned in itself as well as being part of a harmonious whole. Predominantly white or dark surfaces were highlighted by inset coloured glass, gesso plaster panels, delicate light fittings or stencilled patterns.

The monument on the seafront commemorates **Henry Bell** (1767-1830), the designer of the first steamboat *The Comet*, which operated on the Clyde between 1812 and 1820.

The road follows the eastern shores of Gare Loch and Loch Long, favourite waters for sailing. The villages along their banks are good sailing centres (Rhu, Garelochhead, Kilcreggan and Arrochar).

Arrochar – Population 477. This village at the head of Loch Long is a favoured climbing centre nestling at the foot of the Arrochar Alps, Bens Ime, Vane and Arthur or the Cobbler, all of which are about 3 000ft/900m.

The next part of the itinerary goes through the **Argyll Forest Park**, the first of its kind to be established in 1935. The forest park covers 100sq mi/25 000ha of scenic territory on the Cowal Peninsula between lochs Fyne and Long. A variety of forest roads and recreational facilities are open to the public.

The forested valley sides of Glen Croe are overlooked by the slopes of Ben Arthur, more popularly known as the Cobbler (2 891ft/881m).

The Rest and be Thankful – 860ft/262m. This windy pass is the main gateway to Argyll. It took its name from a stone seat which carried this inscription but which has now vanished.

Once through Glen Kinglas branch left by A 815 towards Dunoon.

The road has good views of Loch Fyne, over to Inveraray on the opposite bank.

At Strachur continue on A 815 which goes inland, following the shores of landlocked Loch Eck to cross to the opposite side of the Cowal Peninsula.

Younger Botanic Garden, Benmore – *Outstation of the Royal Botanic Garden, Edinburgh*. This woodland garden in its attractive mountain setting, is renowned for its conifers and its rhododendron and azalea collection. The main flowering season is from the end of April to early June.

Dunoon – Population 8 797. Facilities. This popular seaside resort on the Firth of Clyde is the setting each August for the **Cowal Highland Gathering** and the Pipe Band Championship. The town makes a good centre for touring the Cowal Peninsula and visiting other Clyde resorts by steamer during the high season. Car ferries to Gourock offer a short cut out or an alternative return route.

The Clyde Estuary: south shore to Rothesay using the car ferry – *31mi/50km, 1hr excluding visiting times and ferry. Leave Glasgow by M 8 in the direction of Greenock.*

Port Glasgow – Population 21 554. The town of New Port of Glasgow grew up around the port and harbour facilities built in the 17C by the burgesses of Glasgow, to handle the trade which up until then had passed via the Ayrshire ports. Port Glasgow is still an active shipbuilding centre. Down on the waterfront amid warehouses and shipyards, stands a 16C mansion, **Newark Castle**. It was actually on land bought from a 17C owner that the new port was established. A 15C gatehouse and tower house are linked by 16C buildings to form ranges on three sides of a courtyard. The interest of the exterior is at roof level with the interplay between corbelled turrets, crow-stepped gables, ornamented dormers and tall chimneys. The detailing on the courtyard fronts is concentrated on the pediments and door surround. Inside, the stairs rise in straight flights to the first floor where the hall has a splendid Renaissance fireplace and in two of the apartments there are remains of 16C painted ceilings.

Greenock – Population 57 324. This important shipbuilding centre was the birthplace of **James Watt** (1736-1819), a pioneer in the development of the steam engine. Lyle Hill, behind the town, provides an excellent vantage point, affording a wide **view★★** of the Clyde estuary from Helensburgh right round to Dunoon. Nearby is the memorial, in the form of a Lorraine Cross and anchor combined, to the Free French Naval Forces who lost their lives between 1940 and 1945.

Gourock – Population 11 087. A continuation of Greenock, this Clyde resort is the railway and ferry terminal for Dunoon.

Wemyss Bay – Population 1 513. Wemyss Bay is still the mainland railhead for Rothesay on the Isle of Bute and still has its magnificent Italianate-cum-Tudor **station** built by the Caledonian Railway in 1903, the finest of its kind in Scotland.

Part of the River Clyde's industrial heritage

Rothesay – *Bute.* Population 5 408. Facilities. Another of the Clyde resorts, Rothesay is Bute's only town. The imposing waterfront dates from Rothesay's heyday as a spa. The safe waters of Rothesay Bay are a base for Clyde yachtsmen. **Rothesay Castle** is an early example of a castle of enclosure. The great circular curtain wall is encircled by a water-filled moat and quartered by four round towers, two of which are reduced to their foundations. One has been partially transformed into a dovecot. The forework addition contains the great hall and in the courtyard there is a ruined chapel.

Mount Stuart – *Southeast of Rothesay, Bute.* On a beautiful stretch of sandy shoreline backed by the Argyll hills, on the site of an early-18C house destroyed by fire, rises an imposing Victorian mansion built by R Rowand Anderson for the 3rd Marquess of Bute (1847-1900), a renowned scholar and mystic with a passion for architecture.

A spectacular star-studded **vaulted ceiling***** crowns the vast arcaded main **hall** which boasts a profusion of decorative elements: columns in rare polychrome marble, capitals decorated with naturalistic flowers in white marble, rich stained-glass windows, gilt-bronze balustrade. Mirrors at the back of the arcades enhance the overall effect and a fine collection of portraits illustrates the family history. Also of special interest are the chapel in gleaming white marble, the ornate horoscope room, the elegant drawing-room (coffered ceiling decorated with the family tree) and the large library. The woodlands and landscaped gardens are planted with exotic species.

Summerlee Heritage Park – *Coatbridge. 9mil14km from the city centre, east by M 8 and A 89.* The museum is housed in the converted ironworks on the bank of the Monkland Canal. The displays illustrate the industrial activities which brought prosperity to the country as well as the living conditions of the workers and their families. ■

LOCH LOMOND★★

Argyll and Bute and Stirling

Michelin Atlas p 55 or Map 501 – G 15

The legendary beauty of the "Queen of Scottish Lochs", so often celebrated in song and verse, is one of blue waters flanked by shapely mountains or fringed by more pastoral wooded shores. The loch is 23mi/37km long and 5mi/8km at its widest and has a maximum depth of 653ft/200m. The water discharges into the Firth of Clyde by the River Leven and up to the 13C the loch was known by the same name. It was only later that it took the name of the prominent ben on its eastern shore.

The ruggedly mountainous scenery of the narrow northern end changes in the south to a more pastoral setting of wooded islands and shores.

Only 20mi/32km from the centre of Glasgow the shores are popular for day outings. It is advisable to avoid the weekends, as traffic on the busy west shore road is often nose to tail. For the energetic, part of the West Highland Way *(see Index)* from Glasgow to Fort William follows the east shore.

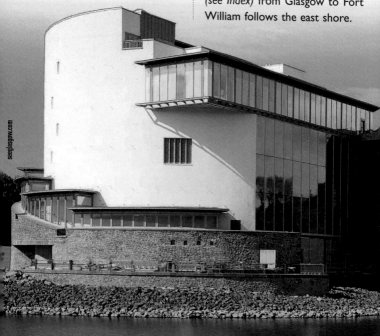

Boat trip – By far the best way to discover the charms of Loch Lomond is to take the pleasure boat, which leaves from Balloch bridge, and calls at Luss, Rowardennan, Tarbet and Inversnaid.

■ Sites and towns

Balloch – Population 5 771. Boat trips leave from this resort. **Loch Lomond Shores** Visitor Centre offers shops, restaurants and tourist information.

Inchmurrin – The largest of the 30 or so islands speckling the wider southern part of the loch. At the southern tip are the ruins of what was once a Lennox stronghold.

Inchcailloch – Nature Reserve. Balmaha marks the passage of the Highland Boundary Fault where mountains suddenly rise out of lowlands.

Luss* – Population 256. A highly attractive village with mellow coloured-stone cottages.

Beyond Luss the loch narrows and the mountains close in.

Rowardennan – The loch's eastern road ends at Rowardennan, now a youth hostel. A path leads from the pier to the summit of Ben Lomond.

Ben Lomond** – The shapely form of this 3 192ft/974m peak rises on the east shore behind Rowardennan. This is the most southerly of the Highland Munros *(see Index)*.

On a level with Tarbet, the dramatic pile of Ben Arthur (2 891ft/881m), better known as the Cobbler, rises in the distance.

Tarbet – Population 257. Tarbet lies at the head of a short valley which leads southwestwards to Arrochar. The Vikings are said to have hauled their galleys over this neck of land to claim sovereignty over the peninsula.

Inversnaid – See The TROSSACHS. From here there is a splendid **view**, across the loch, of the mountains on the far shore: left to right the craggy shaped **Cobbler**, then a group of four, A'Chrois, Beinn Ime (3 318ft/1 011m) and Chorranach further back with Ben Vane rising from the lochside. ■

Lomond Shores,
near Balloch

THE TROSSACHS★★★

Stirling

Michelin Atlas p 55 or Map 501 – G15
See plans below

One of Scotland's most famous beauty spots, the Trossachs conjures up an idyllic landscape of great scenic beauty where rugged, but not so lofty mountains, and their wooded slopes, are reflected in the sparkling waters of the lochs.

"So wondrous and wild, the whole might seem

The scenery of a fairy dream."

The Trossachs proper are delimited by the head of Loch Achray in the east, the foot of Loch Katrine to the west, Ben An (1 750ft/533m) to the north and Ben Venue (2 393ft/727m) to the south. The term is now more generally taken to cover a wider area reaching from Loch Venachar in the east to the shores of Loch Lomond.

Proximity to the great urban populations of Edinburgh, Glasgow and the Central Valley, combined with ease of accessibility, makes this a most popular area with locals and tourists alike. To appreciate to the full the solitude and scenic splendours, it is advisable to visit early in the morning when the coaches are not yet about and driving on the narrow roads is still a pleasure.

Queen Elizabeth Forest Park – As early as 1794, planned forestry was being practised in the vicinity of Lochs Ard and Chon with tanning, building materials and fuel as the main products. In 1928 the Forestry Commission purchased land south of Loch Ard, the initial step in the creation of the Queen Elizabeth Forest Park. Designated as such in 1953, the park has 32 000 acres of plantations out of its total 41 973 acres. Loch Ard, Achray and Rowardennan forests stretch from the Trossachs proper to the eastern shore of Loch Lomond. The great tourist popularity of the area emphasises the importance of the Forestry Commission's role in maintaining a balance between recreation and conservation. For amenities provided within the Forest Park's boundaries, see the Forest Park Visitor Centre.

Excursions – The area described here under the heading Trossachs has been intentionally extended towards Loch Lomond in the west and in the south to the Lake of Menteith for the convenience of the round tour described below, which has Callander as its starting point. An alternative day tour combining boat and bus trips covers the western part of the area, starting from Balloch.

■ Round tour starting from Callander

59 miles – allow a day including visits and boat trip – local map see below

Callander*

Known to millions as the Tannochbrae of *Dr Finlay's Casebook*, Callander is a busy summer resort on the banks of the River Teith. Astride one of the principal routes into the Highlands, the town was built on Drummond lands confiscated after the 18C Jacobite risings. Its popularity has grown ever since, owing in large part to its proximity to the Trossachs.

Leave Callander by A 84 in the direction of Crianlarich (Lochearnhead). After 1mi/1.5km branch left to take The Trossachs road, A 821.

This road climbs up with the great shoulder of **Ben Ledi** (2 882ft/ 879m) on the right. On looking backwards Callander can be seen nestling in the valley floor. As the road moves round the lower slopes of Ben Ledi, it approaches **Loch Venachar** (4mi/6.5km long; *parking and picnic places*).

Brig o'Turk – This widely scattered village at the mouth of Glen Finglas is closely associated with the Ruskins and Millais who spent an extended holiday in the area in 1853. Brig o'Turk was one of the early summer haunts of the Glasgow Boys *(see Index)*. James Guthrie's *Highland Funeral (Art*

A land of romance and adventure

Much of the rugged terrain of the Trossachs was MacGregor country and is closely associated with the daring exploits of Rob Roy MacGregor (1671-1734), an outlaw and the leader of the MacGregor Clan, which Sir Walter Scott recounted in Rob Roy (1818).

Sir Walter was instrumental in popularising the Trossachs with his romantic poem, *The Lady of the Lake*. Such was the public desire to follow in the footsteps of Scott's fictional characters that the Duke of Montrose built **Duke's Road** in 1820, a connecting road north from Aberfoyle.

Other famous visitors included the Wordsworths and Coleridge in 1830 following which Wordsworth wrote *To a Highland Girl*.

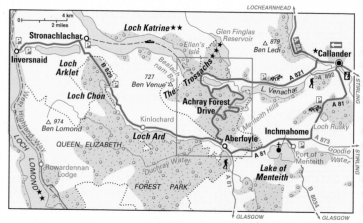

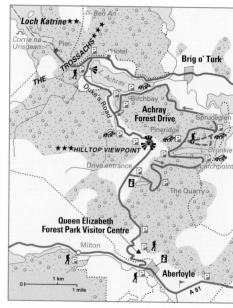

Key:

🖼 Picnic site

🚶 Forest walk

Gallery and Museum Kelvingrove, Glasgow) depicts an episode of the period.

Once across the Finglas Water the road enters the **Achray Forest**, part of the Queen Elizabeth Forest Park. After the initial discovery of a smaller loch, Loch Achray, only passing glimpses can be had of this, while the second great peak of the area, **Ben Venue** (2 393ft/727m), stands out in the distance with the white form of Loch Achray Hotel at its feet. Pass on the right the castellated 20C reconstruction of the Trossachs Hotel, originally named Drunkie Hotel and renamed after a visit by Queen Victoria. At the end of the Loch, the road continues on to Loch Katrine (dead end).

Loch Katrine★★ – *1mi/1.5km from A 821 to the pier and car park. No access round loch for vehicles.* Other than hill walking, the only but very rewarding way to discover this famous loch is to take a **boat trip** on the SS *Sir Walter Scott*.

The loch (10mi/16km long and 2mi/3.2km at its widest) has been Glasgow's water supply since 1859, when Queen Victoria officiated at the inauguration. On the north-eastern slopes of the twin-peaked Ben Venue are Corrie na Urisgean (Goblin's Cave), the traditional meeting place of Scotland's goblins, and Bealach nam Bo (Pass of the Cattle), a route much favoured by the drover Rob Roy when returning home with cattle. Ellen's Isle (Eilean Molach) figures in Scott's *The Lady of the Lake*.

The boat turns about at Stronachlachar from where a road leads westwards to Inversnaid on the shores of Loch Lomond. Glen Gyle, at the head of Loch Katrine, was the birthplace of Rob Roy and on the north shore is a MacGregor burial place. Factor's Isle, another Rob Roy haunt, is where the outlaw held the Duke of Montrose's factor, Baillie Nicol Jarvie, in reprisal for having evicted Rob Roy's family.

Return to the junction with A 821 and take Duke's Road, in the Aberfoyle direction, to pass round the head of Loch Achray.

From level with the **car park** there is a good view up the loch. Once round to the south side the road climbs with good views over Loch Achray.

Hilltop viewpoint★★★ – *Park at the roadside; 5min climb to viewing-table.* There is an excellent **panorama**★★★ of the Trossachs, encompassing Ben Venue, Loch Katrine with its mountain ring, Ben An, Finglas Reservoir, Ben Ledi with Brig o'Turk at its feet, Loch Venachar and due east round to the Menteith Hills. In the immediate foreground is Loch Drunkie in the heart of Achray Forest.

Achray Forest Drive – This forest road (7mi/11km long) makes an excellent outing for those wanting an afternoon away from it all *(ample parking and picnic places with a choice of walks)* but since it is through forested countryside it has few views of the surrounding countryside.

Away on the right can be seen scars of now disused slate quarries.

Queen Elizabeth Forest Park Visitor Centre – *Information centre for park amenities open to the public.* The audio-visual presentation is an excellent introduction to the for-

The Fairy Folk

Local folklore includes such supernatural creatures as the Water Bull of Loch Katrine and the Water Horse of Loch Venachar. An Aberfoyle minister, the Reverend Robert Kirk, committed to print their secrets in *The Secret Commonwealth of Elfs, Fawns and Fairies* (1691) following a prolonged stay with the fairies. Another more humorous tale is that of the first commercial venture to ply the waters of Loch Katrine with a steamboat, *The Water Witch*. The offending boat sank to tales of goblins and monsters, and the Highlanders' oared-galley trade continued to flourish.

est park. A variety of **trails** are open to the public including the Fairy Trail centred on Doon Hill, the site from where the Rev Robert Kirk was spirited away by the fairy folk.

The road then descends into Aberfoyle leaving behind the mountainous rim of the Central Highlands.

Aberfoyle – Population 546. A clachan in the time of Rob Roy, Aberfoyle was made famous as the meeting place of Rob and Nicol Jarvie. Today it is busy with tourists in summer, many of whom throng the sales floor of **The Scottish Wool Centre**. Here, in addition to the merchandise, the Story of Scottish Wool is told by means of an entertaining "sheep show", where the models all have four legs.

Leave Aberfoyle to the west by B 829, a single track road.

This **scenic road**, ending beside Inversnaid Hotel on Loch Lomond makes a pleasant drive through the southwestern part of the Queen Elizabeth Forest Park.

Loch Ard – The road along the north shore runs close to the water's edge of Loch Ard described by Queen Victoria in 1869 as "a fine long loch with trees of all kinds overhanging the road, heather making all pink, bracken, rocks, high hills of such fine shape and trees growing up them as in Switzerland. Altogether the whole view was lovely". The **scenery** has lost none of its attraction with the southern shore clothed with the trees of Loch Ard Forest. The prominent outline of Ben Lomond looms large on the horizon. There is a fine **view** of Loch Chon backed by the 'Arrochar Alps' in the distance.

Loch Chon – This is the smaller of the two lochs.

At the road junction the branch to the right leads to Stronachlachar.

Stronachlachar – On the south shore of Loch Katrine. The *SS Sir Walter Scott* makes a stop at this point.

Return to the junction and carry straight on.

Loch Arklet – *Reservoir, no access to the water's edge.* This artificial loch lies in a glacially created hanging valley.

The ruins to the right are those of Inversnaid barracks built in the early 18C to curb the Mac-Gregors.

Inversnaid – On Loch Lomond-side, the hotel overlooks the pier, one of the stopping places of the steamer cruises. The far side of Loch Lomond *(see LOCH LO-MOND)* is dominated by the peaks of the Cobbler, Bens Vorlich, Vane and Ime. The **West Highland Way** follows this shore of Loch Lomond, on its way north to Fort William.

Return towards Aberfoyle, leaving to the east. At the junction with A 81 turn left.

The road skirts the great rounded spine of the Menteith Hills.

Lake of Menteith – On the northern edge of Flanders Moss, the lake is one of the venues for the national bonspiel, the Grand Match between north and south, organised by the Royal Caledonian Curling Club.

Pass the lake and then turn right in the direction of Arnprior. The car park is 0.5mi/800m down the road.

Inchmahome Priory – *This is an island monastery. To attract the ferryman's attention when he is on the island, turn the white board on the jetty.* The mid-13C ruins include the church of the Augustinian priory with its deeply recessed west doorway strongly resembling the one at Dunblane and the chapter-house which shelters an unusual **double effigy*** tomb monument. Mary, Queen of Scots spent some time here in 1547 prior to embarking for France.

Return to Callander by A 81. ∎

BOTHWELL CASTLE*

South Lanarkshire

Michelin Atlas p 55 or Map 501 – H 16

The ruins of Both-
well Castle the most
outstanding 13C
fortress, remain impressive in their
commanding site high above the
Clyde Valley. This castle, of roughly
the same period as Edward I's Welsh
strongholds, is one of a group in
Scotland (Kildrummy, Tantallon and
Dirleton) showing a decided European influence in defensive design.

A much disputed stronghold
– Built in the late 13C by a
member of the Moravia family,
the castle figured largely in the
Wars of Independence. It fell into
English hands in 1301 and on being retaken in 1314 after Bannock-
burn, it suffered a first dismantling.
The castle was repaired during a
second period of English occupation when Edward III made it his
headquarters in 1336. By the next
year the Scots were again in com-
mand and under the "scorched
earth" policy Bothwell was again
dismantled. The castle lay in ruin
until it passed by marriage to
Archibald the Grim, the 3rd Earl
of Douglas, in 1362 and he made
this his chief residence. The late
14C and early 15C saw further
additions and embellishments.
Following the Douglas forfeiture
of 1445, the castle passed through

several hands before becoming the property of Patrick Hepburn, Lord Hailes, who exchanged it for Hermitage with the Red Douglas, Archibald, 5th Earl of Angus.

Castle ruins – The first impression on seeing this red sandstone ruin, all towers and curtain walls, is one of sheer size and yet only part of the original 13C plan was executed. The initial frontage was to have been a gatehouse flanked by drum towers with curtain walls receding to the present construction.

Take the stairs in the northeast tower to reach the courtyard enclosure. At the far end, the oldest and most impressive part, the 13C circular **keep** or donjon, designed to serve as the last bastion of defence, shows "masterly design and stonework". The keep itself is protected by a moat on the courtyard side, with the drawbridge giving access to the doorway, sheltering behind a beak construction. Walled up following partial dismantling, three storeys and a fighting level rise above the basement. The tower communicates with the 13C prison tower and postern in the south curtain wall. In the southeast corner, the early-15C chapel, marked at first floor level by two pointed windows, communicates with the other great four storey tower, also 15C. Beyond, against the east curtain wall, above cellars, is the **great hall** with its succession of elegant windows.

Walk round the outside to appreciate the setting, the site, the dimensions and the fine masonry of the 13C parts.

Bothwell – Population 4 840. The town grew up in the shadow of its great castle at an important bridging point on the Clyde. Bothwell developed rapidly in the 19C when it was favoured by wealthy Glasgow merchants. A memorial beside Bothwell Bridge (north bank) commemorates the **battle** of 1679 when the Covenanters suffered their worst defeat. 400 were killed and 1 200 taken prisoner. ∎

HAMILTON

South Lanarkshire

Population 51 529
Michelin Atlas p 55 or Map 501 – H16

Seat of the powerful Hamilton family, premier dukes of Scotland, the town changed its name from Cadzow to Hamilton in the 15C and became a royal burgh a century later in 1548. The town grew rapidly in the late 18C and early 19C as a centre of the coal mining industry with the discovery and exploitation of Lanarkshire coal seams. Today Hamilton is a busy shopping and administrative centre.

Hamilton Low Parks Museum – *129 Muir Street*. This former coaching inn includes the 18C Assembly Room and houses a local history collection, a transport section and displays illustrating local industries of the past, notably lacemaking. Samples of both lace periods are on display: the 17C bobbin lace introduced by the Duchess Anne and the 19C tambour lace.

Cameronians (Scottish Rifles) Regimental Museum – *Behind the museum*. This museum occupies the Duke of Hamilton's old riding school. The 279 years of the now disbanded regiment's history are illustrated by displays of uniforms, medals, banners and commemorative photographs.

Hamilton Mausoleum – *Low Parks*. Alexander, 10th Duke of Hamilton (1767-1852), known as El Magnifico, commissioned this imposing building which took 15 years to build (1842-57). The duke himself was buried in 1852 in an Egyptian sarcophagus. The mausoleum is famed for its echo which prevented it being used as a chapel as intended.

Chatelherault – *High Parks. Chatelherault Country Park off A 74 south of Hamilton. Leave the car in the car park beside the adventure playground.* The imposing "Dogg Kennell" is a reminder of the once magnificent Hamilton Palace (1822-1927), the grandiose ducal seat. Its magnificence surpassed all bounds with a superb collection of paintings and furniture. Sold by auction in 1862, the palace was demolished in 1927 because of subsidence due to mining.

The 5th Duke commissioned William Adam to build a lodge for hunting parties and a "dogg kennell" which was to be the focal point for the palace's grand avenue. It stands on the edge of the River Avon gorge near the Hamilton's original seat of Cadzow Castle.

The **visitor centre** has an audio-visual presentation giving an introduction to the palace, lodge, country park and its wildlife and amenities. Arranged around the courtyard, the interpretative centre (formerly the kennels, gun room, slaughter house with game larder) comprises a series of talking tableaux which introduce the visitor to several 18C estate workers (the master of the hounds, forester, stonemason and head gardener).

On the way to visit the garden, stop to admire the prospect northwards to where Hamilton Palace would have stood, in front of the mausoleum (see above). Part of the grand avenue has been replanted.

The **house** used for hunting parties has been refurbished and the magnificent ceilings recreated. The originals were by Thomas Clayton (fl 1710-60), the foremost craftsman plasterer of his day who also worked at Blair Castle, Hopetoun House and Holyroodhouse. The ceilings in the banqueting hall and the duke's room are attractively elaborate.

Other features within the park's boundaries are the ruins of Cadzow Castle on the other bank of the Avon Gorge and a herd of white cattle with distinctive black markings on the muzzle, ears and around the eyes. This ancient breed is quite rare. ■

S. Chraïbi/©ACSI

KILMARNOCK

East Ayrshire

Population 52 080
Michelin Atlas p 55 or Map 501 – G 17

Lying in the heart of the Ayrshire countryside, Kilmarnock is the area's premier shopping town. Main industries include whisky blending and carpet making.

■ Sights

Dean Castle – *Off Glasgow Road.* The grounds are now a country park. The castle was for long the seat of the Boyd family. Following a fire in the 18C it stood empty prior to a complete restoration in the 20C. In the 14C **keep**, the main halls, hung with 15C-16C Flemish tapestries, are the setting for two small but exceptionally rich medieval collections. In the great hall, the mainly 16C **arms and armour★** display includes pieces of outstanding craftsmanship, all finely decorated. Upstairs in the solar are early **musical instruments★** of Italian, French and German origin, all decoratively painted, inlaid or carved. Outstanding are the 17C Italian spinet supported by its gilt figure and the 16C and early-17C lutes and guitars.

Dick Institute – *Elmbank Avenue.* The library, museum and art gallery are under one roof. On the first floor the museum includes extensive geological and natural history sections. Note the Lochlea Crannog (lake dwelling) exhibit. The more specialised collection of **basket-hilted swords** has examples of both Scottish and foreign craftsmanship. Great skill and artistry were lavished on the elaboration of the openwork baskets. The paintings of the permanent collection are displayed in rotation and include works by Corot, Teniers, Constable, Millais and the Scottish School. ■

LANARK

Population 9 673
Michelin Atlas p 55 or Map 501 – I 16

This busy market town has one of the biggest livestock markets in Scotland. The town has William Wallace *(see Index)* associations and what is supposedly the oldest racing trophy, The Silver Bell. Festivals include the Lanimer Festival with the traditional riding of the marches and the unusual "Whuppity Scourie" ceremony which promises to banish winter.

■ **New Lanark**★★ *2hr*

New Lanark down on the floor of the deep gorge of the River Clyde, is a good example of an 18C planned industrial village. When the Glasgow tobacco trade collapsed owing to the American War of Independence (1776-83) cotton manufacturing was quick to take its place exploiting a workforce skilled in linen making.

In 1783, a Glasgow manufacturer and banker, **David Dale** (1736-1806), brought Richard Arkwright, inventor of the spinning power frame, to the area to prospect suitable sites for a new factory. The present site was chosen and the smallest of the Falls of Clyde

harnessed to provide water power for the mills. Building started in 1785 and by 1799 the four mills and associated housing comprised Scotland's largest cotton mill supporting a village population of over 2 000.

In 1800 Dale sold the mills to his future son-in-law, **Robert Owen** (1771-1858) the social reformer, who took over as managing partner and was to remain for 25 years. The mills were a commercial success enabling Owen to put a series of social experiments into practice. He created the Nursery Buildings, the Institute for the Formation of Character, the village store and school. **Owenism** was widely acclaimed in that age of increasing industrialisation but was eclipsed by government and employer resistance.

Cotton continued to be manufactured here until 1968. A major restoration programme is now in progress. In 1986, the village was nominated a World Heritage Site.

Village – *The best approach is on foot from the car park. Stop on way down at viewpoint with orientation table.* The centrepiece, **New Buil-**

dings (1798), pinpointed by the bell tower is prolonged to the right by the **Nursery Buildings** (1809) to house the pauper apprentices who worked and usually lived in the mills, and then the cooperative **store** (1810) – now refurbished with an exhibition about Owen's original store and a period-style shop. The bow-ended **counting house** terminates a line of restored tenements which took its name, **Caithness Row,** from the storm-bound Highlanders on their way to America who were accommodated and subsequently settled here.

At the other end of the village, beyond Dale and Owen's houses, is more tenement housing, while between the river and the lade stands the massive **mill** comprising three units. The fourth mill was destroyed by fire in 1883.

The most handsome of all is **mill n° 3** the only one to have been rebuilt by Owen in 1826. Mill 1 was fully reconstructed in 1995 and has been converted recently into a luxury hotel. The engine house gives access to a new glass bridge – to the pattern of the original rope-race – which in turn leads to mill 3 with exhibition space, audio-visual presentation (Visions of the Millennium) and visitor facilities. The architecture of this fireproof structure is best viewed from the ramp hall. Adjoining the engine house is the **Institute**, a social and recreational centre of the village while the school (after restoration it will become an educational centre with modern facilities) stands further back. A Millworker's House shows living conditions of the 1820s and 1930s.

The **Dyeworks**, by the river, serve as a Scottish Wildlife Trust visitor centre with an audio-visual show and displays on the wildlife of the Falls of Clyde Reserve.

Falls of Clyde – *From New Lanark a riverside path leads*

New Lanark

upstream to the gorge section of the Clyde with its series of falls, now harnessed by a hydroelectric scheme. This stretch of river with the three sets of falls, was once one of Scotland's most visited beauty spots. The Falls were portrayed variously by Turner, Paul Sandby and Jacob More and described by Wordsworth, Coleridge and Scott.

In spite of a lack of bathing naiads, and even water at times, this wooded stretch of the Clyde retains a certain charm. A viewpoint beyond Bonnington Power Station provides an excellent **view** of the highest falls, **Corra Linn** where the drop is 60ft/18m. These become spectacular on open days when the water is turned on and thunders over the rocky lips down to a boiling mass below with a pall of vapour hanging above.

■ Excursion

Craignethan Castle – *5mi/8km northwest by A 72. Turn left on the far side of Crossford.* Sir James Hamilton of Finnart (1512-71), Master of Works to James V and natural son of the 1st Earl of Arran, built this attractive biscuit-coloured tower house with its double courtyard. The original stronghold stands on a promontory with steep slopes on three sides while the vulnerable fourth side overlooked by high ground is protected by a dry ditch and an outer courtyard.

Built between 1530 and 1540, this castle *(restoration work in progress)* has the distinction of being designed for defence against artillery. In the right-hand corner of the first courtyard is a 17C dwelling (curator's house) built by the Covenanter **Andrew Hay.** On the floor of the dry ditch separating the two courtyards is a unique defensive feature, a **caponier** or vaulted gallery. A tall curtain wall (5ft/1.5m thick) originally rose behind the ditch and access to the inner courtyard was by a gateway round to the left. The tower house with its two storeys is squat by normal standards, probably not rising above the curtain which preceded it. ■

LARGS

North Ayrshire

Population 9 619
Michelin Atlas p 54 or Map 501 – F 16 – Facilities

Largs is a popular Ayrshire coast resort, much frequented by Glaswegians, with ample accommodation and the usual range of amenities.

The town was the site of the **Battle of Largs** (1263), an inconclusive affair during the reign of Alexander III. The Norwegian King Haakon was on a summer expedition to his foreign territories of the Western Isles and Isle of Man when his fleet was blown ashore at Largs, with the ensuing battle. Haakon died at Kirkwall on the return journey. A monument on the shore to the south of the town, the **Viking Festival**, and Vikingar! *(see below)* commemorate this battle. Three years later by the Treaty of Perth, the Norwegians renounced all claims to the Western Isles, although retaining Orkney and Shetland. Relations so improved between the two nations that Alexander's daughter, Margaret, married King Eric in 1281.

Largs Old Kirk★ – *Old Kirkyard, off Main Street.* Originally the north transept of a larger church, the **Skelmorlie aisle** was transformed into a mausoleum by Sir Robert Montgomery in 1636. The refined but stark simplicity of the exterior gives no hint of the inner splendours. The elegant canopied **Renaissance monument** is a mass of fine sculptural detail akin to the decorative work at Argyll's Lodging, Stirling. The coffered design of the **painted ceiling** frames heraldic devices, signs of the Zodiac, the seasons and ornate Italianate patterns. In the winter scene note the players of golf or kolf.

Vikingar! – In the resort's ultra-modern leisure centre, Vikingar! is a thrilling multimedia experience which vividly evokes the Vikings'

Golf in Inverclyde

way of life, their cosmology, and their warrior ethic, culminating in the Battle of Largs.

Clyde Muirshiel Regional Park – The uplands rising abruptly above Largs are protected and made accessible to the public as one of Scotland's four Regional Parks. The area (100sq mi/260km^2) has woods, glens, lochs, a rich and varied wildlife, and offers magnificent views over the Clyde and the mountains beyond. Just to the south of Largs and within the boundary of the Regional Park, **Kelburn Castle and Country Centre** offers a range of family attractions, including walking, riding, falconry, tours of the castle mansion, and visits to the "Secret Forest".

■ Excursions

Great Cumbrae – The island's main town, **Millport**, strung out round the head of Millport Bay is much favoured by Glasgow holidaymakers. 1mi/1.5km out of town is the **University Marine Biological Station**.

This scientific research centre has a small but interesting exhibition explaining the geology and marine conformation of the Clyde Sea Area and work of the station.

Specimens of the various local species are to be found in the adjoining **aquarium** (13 tanks).

The island affords the best view of the industrial complex on the mainland at Hunterston Sands.

Hunterston Nuclear Power Station – *5mi/8km south by A 78.* This is part of an industrial zone south of Largs, beyond the residential and now flourishing holiday resort of **Fairlie**, world famous for its yacht building yards. Famous examples included the various *Shamrock* yachts built for the founder of the tea empire and enthusiastic yachtsman, Sir Thomas Lipton (1850-1931). Lipton was runner-up five times in his bid to win the America's Cup.

Hunterston sits on a promontory, sheltered by the Cumbraes. Hunterston A was Scotland's first commercial nuclear power station after the experimental one at Dounreay. Opened in 1964 this was one of the first generation Magnox Reactors. Three years later work started on Hunterston B, an advanced gas-cooled reactor (AGR), and power was first produced in 1976. Together these nuclear stations play a vital role in supplying Scotland's electricity. ■

PAISLEY

Renfrewshire

Population 84 330
Michelin Atlas p 55 or Map 501 – G16

The industrial town of Paisley, long famed for its Paisley shawls and thread production, now has a more highly diversified industrial sector although thread production still plays an important role. The village, which grew up around the 12C monastic establishment, expanded in the 18C owing to linen manufacturing.

Cradle of the Stewarts – David I granted lands and the hereditary position of High Steward to Walter Fitzalan. **Walter Stewart** (1292-1326), the 6th High Steward, married Marjory Bruce who died giving birth to their son, the future Robert II, the first Stewart king. The **Royal House of Stewart** (later Stuart), despite James V's prophecy, did not end with Mary, Queen of Scots but continued to rule until the 17C. Twelve Stuarts reigned for over 300 years and four occupied the English throne. The male line ceased in 1807 with the death of Prince Henry Benedict, Cardinal York. HRH The Prince Charles is the 29th Lord High Steward of Scotland.

Famous sons – **John Wilson** (1785-1854) alias Christopher North, the poet, essayist, contributor to the *Blackwood Magazine* and Professor of Moral Philosophy at Edinburgh, was a contemporary of Scott and firm friend of James Hogg "the Ettrick Shepherd" *(see Index)* and Thomas de Quincey. The latter figures in his masterpiece, *Noctes Ambrosianae*, a series of imaginary colloquies in an Edinburgh tavern. Paisley was also the birthplace of the poet weaver, **Robert Tannahill** (1774-1810), and the ornithologist and poet **Alexander Wilson** (1766-1813). Originally a weaver also, Wilson emigrated to America where his work on North American birds influenced America's own John J Audubon.

■ Sights

Paisley Abbey – Walter Fitzalan founded a priory in 1163 bringing monks from the Cluniac establishment at Wenlock. Elevated to abbey in 1245, the monastery became one of the richest and most powerful in Scotland.

Although the priory was a 12C foundation, the present-day church is mostly 15C and the result of many rebuildings and extensive restorations. In the heart of Paisley, the church is an impressive sight as it stands unencumbered by encroaching buildings. The deeply recessed west front **doorway** is 13C Early Pointed Gothic. Inside, the corbelled galleries at the clerestory level of the nave are unusual in that they go round the outside of the pillars. The St Mirin Chapel, in the south transept, commemorates St Columba's friend and contemporary. The long choir, a 19C and 20C restoration, has Robert Lorimer furnishings. Here also is the tomb reputed to be that of Marjory Bruce, wife of the 6th High Steward of Scotland (see above).

Paisley shawls

When the fashion for imitation Kashmir shawls developed in 18C Europe, Paisley was not one of the initial centres (Edinburgh and Norwich) to manufacture such goods. It was in 1805 that an Edinburgh manufacturer introduced the art to Paisley, where it prospered, initially as a cottage industry. Such was the success that all patterned shawls with the traditional "pine" motifs came to be known as **Paisley shawls**. In early examples, decorated end pieces and borders with two or three colours were sewn onto plain centres, which were later covered with a small motif. With the introduction of the Jacquard loom (1820s), the industry became more factory based, and intricate overall patterns with as many as 10 colours were popular. Printed shawls were introduced in the 1840s and were followed in the 1860s by the reversible shawl which never gained any real popularity.

The local museum has an excellent collection, demonstrating all the beauty and intricacy of these multicoloured, fine garments which were appreciated equally for their warmth, lightness and softness.

The **Place of Paisley** is all that remains of the monastic buildings which, after the Reformation, were appropriated as the commendator's residence.

Paisley Museum and Art Gallery – *High Street.* This 19C building, one of the Coats bequests, houses a series of well displayed collections. The comprehensive **Paisley Shawl Section*** outlines the development of this specialised local activity and includes examples of its varied products *(see above for more details).* The art gallery

has a number of works by the Scottish School (Gillies, Walton and George Henry). Other sections include a good pottery collection, and local and natural history exhibits. The **Coats Observatory** has displays on astronomy, meteorology and space flight.

■ Excursion

Kilbarchan Weaver's Cottage – *5mi/8km west, off A 737.* This 18C weaver's cottage with its typical interior of the period, is a reminder of the local cottage industry which still reigned supreme at the turn of the last century. Displayed throughout the cottage

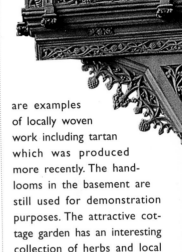

are examples of locally woven work including tartan which was produced more recently. The hand-looms in the basement are still used for demonstration purposes. The attractive cottage garden has an interesting collection of herbs and local historical artefacts. ■

Paisley
Abbey

PRACTICAL INFORMATION

■ Planning a trip ■

Visit Scotland is Scotland's national tourist board. Their head office is at 23 Ravelston Terrace, Edinburgh EH4 3EU ☎ 0131 332 2433; Fax 0131 459 2434; www.visitscotland.com

The **Greater Glasgow & Clyde Valley Tourist Board** is located at 11 George Square, Glasgow G2 1DY ☎ 0141 204 4400; Fax 0141 221 3524; enquiries@seeglasgow.com   It offers an accommodation and theatre booking service. There is also a bureau de change, a tourist information service, a bookshop and a souvenir shop.

Special Needs

Many of the sights described in this guide are accessible to people with special needs. The **Michelin Red Guide Great Britain and Ireland** indicates hotels with facilities suitable for disabled people; it is advisable to book in advance.

■ Getting there ■

By Air

Glasgow International Airport ☎ 0141 887 1111; Fax 0141 849 1444.

Prestwick International Airport (situated 32mi/51km south of Glasgow) ☎ 01292 479 822.

By Rail

Glasgow Central Station (for services to and from England, and with links to Greater Glasgow). Services from London to Glasgow leave from Euston Station.

Glasgow Queen Street Station (for services to and from Edinburgh, and with links to Greater Glasgow)

National Rail Enquiries ☎ 08457 48 49 50

By Coach

National Express operates a regular service between the major towns in the UK and Glasgow. Special discount tickets are available: contact local National Express agents or **National Express** ☎ 08705 80 80 80; www.gobycoach.com

■ Sightseeing ■

Since Glasgow's main sights are well scattered, it is advisable to use public transport (*see below*). City tours in open-topped buses leave from George Square. Audio-guided city walking tours for hire and starting from the Tourist Information Centre.

Clyde Helicopters, City Heliport, SECC, Glasgow ☏ 0141 226 4261 offer helicopter rides which afford spectacular views of the city and of Loch Lomond.

Boat trips "doon the water" along the Firth of Clyde are also very popular in summer. Clyde Marine Cruises, Victoria Harbour, Gourock ☏ 01475 721 281; Fax 01474 888 023; www.clyde-marine.co.uk

Public Transport

The Travel Centre, St Enoch's Square ☏ 0141 332 7133 gives information on travel passes for the underground, bus and trains. The **Underground Heritage Trail** ticket valid for one day allows visitors to discover the varied aspects of Glasgow starting from different metro stations. Information also from **Buchanan Bus Station** ☏ 0141 885 3708.

Car Rental/Hire

The most flexible way of exploring the outskirts of the city is by car. There are car rental agencies at the airports, railway stations and in the city centre.

■ Shopping ■

Sauchiehall, Buchanan and Argyle Streets are pedestrian shopping precincts. The glass-roofed **Princes Square** and **Buchanan** shopping centres in Buchanan Street are pleasant havens where Scottish items are on offer. The **Italian Centre** on the corner of John and Ingram Streets has on sale the finest Italian fashion and also offers bars, brasseries, restaurants and cafés in a beautiful décor.

The **Scottish Craft Centre** in Princes Street displays fine items by Scottish craftsmen which make excellent gifts.

The Barras, a large indoor and outdoor market, is the place to visit not only for a bargain but also for the spectacle.

Outside the city, **Lomond Shores Visitor Centre** in Balloch has an attractive range of luxury outlets with a Scottish theme as well as restaurants and cafés.

■ Entertainment ■

Glasgow has a dynamic cultural scene with avant-garde theatre staged by the Citizens Theatre, the Centre for Contemporary Arts, the Tramway Theatre and the Tron Theatre. Other venues include The Mitchell Theatre, the King's Theatre and the Theatre Royal. Exhibitions are held at the McLellan Galleries, The Third Eye Centre, The Old Fruitmarket and The Lighthouse.

What's On, a monthly publication, lists the shows (theatre, concerts and films) and other events in the Greater Glasgow area. Tickets for most events are on sale at the Ticket Centre, City Hall, Candleriggs.

■ Where to Stay and Where to Eat ■

The **Michelin** Red Guide Great Britain and Ireland is an annual publication which presents a selection of hotels, guesthouses and restaurants. The range is wide, from the modest inn or guesthouse to the most luxurious grand hotel, from the centrally situated modern establishment catering to the needs of business to the secluded or isolated retreat. Places listed in the Red Guide are underlined in red on the Michelin map 501. **Visit Scotland** *(details above)* publishes accommodation brochures.

Booking a room – Visit Scotland and the Tourist Information Centres operate an accommodation booking service for a small booking fee. Room prices, even for a double room, may be quoted per person.

Bed and Breakfast – Many private individuals take in a limited number of guests. Prices include bed and cooked breakfast. Some offer full board or an evening meal but meals tend to be at a set time and the menu may be limited. Many houses advertise with a B&B sign.

University accommodation – During student vacations many universities and colleges offer low-cost accommodation in the halls of residence. Contact **Scottish Universities Accommodation Consortium**, Heriot Watt University, Riccarton, Edinburgh EH14 4AS. ☎ 0131 449 4034; Fax 0131 451 3199.

Youth Hostels – There are many hostels in Scotland. Package holidays are available comprising youth hostel vouchers, rail and bus pass or hostel vouchers, return rail fare and cycle hire. For information apply to:

Scottish Youth Hostels Association, 7 Glebe Crescent, Stirling FK8 2JA. ☎ 01786 891 400; Fax 01786 891 333; syha@syha.org.uk; www.syha.org.uk

British Youth Hostels Association, Trevelyan House, St Albans, Herts AL1 2DY. ☎ 01727 855 215; Fax 01232 439 699. Visitors must hold an international membership card.

Independent Backpackers Hostels – Scotland (I.B.H.S), contact P Thomas, Croft Bunkhouse & Bothies, 7 Portnalong, Isle of Skye IV47 8SL (enclose self-addressed envelope for reply). www.hostel-scotland.co.uk

Camping – Scotland has many officially graded caravan and camping parks with modern facilities and a variety of additional sports facilities. A brochure **Camping and Caravanning** (£3.99), which covers the whole country, is available from the STB.

The two rates quoted for each establishment refer to the nightly rate of a single or double room. Breakfast may not always be included in the price.

Hotels

City Inn, Finnieston Quay, G3 8HN; ☎ 0141 240 1002; glasgow.reservat ions@cityinn.com; £89. Quayside location and views of the Clyde. Well priced hotel with a «business-friendly» ethos; neatly maintained modern rooms with sofas and en suite power showers. Restaurant fronts waterside terrace.

Bewley's, 110 Bath St, G2 2EN; ☎ 0141 353 0800; gla@bewleyshotels.com; £59. A well-run group hotel, relaxed but professional in approach, in the middle of Glasgow's shopping streets. Spacious, affordable accommodation with modern fittings. People-watch from glass-walled brasserie.

Express by Holiday Inn, Theatreland, 165 West Nile St, G1 2RL; ☎ 0141 331 6800; express@higlasgow.com; £69. Modern accommodation – simple and well arranged with adequate amenities. Equally suitable for business travel or short breaks.

Travel Inn Metro, Montrose House, 187 George St, G1 1YU; ☎ 0141 553 2700; £50. Close to George Square and the City Chambers, a former tax office now offering neat, modern rooms at a reasonable price. The restaurant serves a Mediterranean-style menu.

Park House, 13 Victoria Park Gardens South, G11 7BX; ☎ 0141 339 1559; mail@parkhouseglasgow.co.uk; £60-£80. An extensive, smartly kept suburban house retaining much of its Victorian character. Comfortable, classically stylish bedrooms combine period furniture with CD systems. Dining room with neatly set 19C ambience.

Manor Park, 28 Balshagray Drive, G11 7DD; ☎ 0141 339 2143; manorparkhotel@aol.com; £45-£75. A relaxed, homely but dedicated approach is apparent throughout the 19C listed house. Attic rooms are especially spacious: all are comfortable and sympathetically decorated.

The Town House, 4 Hughenden Terr, G12 9XR; ☎ 0141 357 0862; hospitality@thetownhouseglasgow.com; £60-£72. Elegant, personally run town house with fine Victorian plasterwork: spacious, pleasantly decorated rooms and an inviting firelit lounge. Hearty breakfasts.

Kirklee, 11 Kensington Gate, G12 9LG; ☎ 0141 334 5555; kirklee@clara.net; £55-£72. Good-sized, adequately appointed rooms in a peaceful suburban square. Edwardian style summed up by the drawing room's parquet floors, period furniture and tall bay windows.

GLASGOW AIRPORT

Express by Holiday Inn, St Andrews Drive, PA3 2TJ; ☎ 0141 842 1100; info@hiex-glasgow.com; £69. Ideal for both business travellers and families. Spacious, carefully designed, bright and modern bedrooms with plenty of work space. Complimentary continental breakfast. Traditional and busy buffet-style restaurant.

MOTHERWELL

Express by Holiday Inn, Strathclyde Country Park, Hamilton Rd, ML1 3RB; ☎ 01698 858585; £65. Good motorway connections from this purpose-built hotel offering trim rooms in contemporary style plus a small lounge and bar: a useful address for business stopovers.

UDDINGSTON

Redstones, 8-10 Glasgow Rd, G71 7AS; ☎ 01698 813774; redstones1@ aol.com; £65-£185. Renovated Victorian houses in distinctive red sandstone – the conservatory lounge is a later addition; usefully-equipped bedrooms feel stylish and modern. Formally set Le Papillon restaurant. Informal Brooklands dining room just off the bar.

CARDROSS

Kirkton House, Darleith Rd, G82 5EZ; ☎ 01389 841951; mich@ kirktonhouse.co.uk; £50-£79. Former farmhouse with origins in 18C; quiet, elevated spot overlooking North Clyde. Ideal stop-off between Glasgow airport and Highlands. Bedrooms all have country views. Traditional dining room with oil lamps at the tables.

LUSS

Lodge on Loch Lomond, G83 8PA; ☎ 01436 860201; res@loch-lomond.co.uk; £90-£149. Busy family run establishment in a superb spot on the shores of Loch Lomond. Most of the cosy pine panelled rooms have balconies; all of them can boast a sauna. Restaurant and bar lounge carefully designed on two levels, opening the view to every table.

TARBET

Lomond View, G83 7DG; ☎ 01301 702477; lomondview@talk21.com; £50-£70. Purpose-built guesthouse which lives up to its name: there are stunning loch views. Spacious sitting room. Light and airy breakfast room. Sizeable, modern bedrooms.

Pubs

The lively atmosphere of Glasgow pubs is famous: **Rab Ha's** in Hutcheson Street, **Times Square** in St Enoch's Square, **Jock Tamson's** and **Bonhams** in Byres Road and **Dows** in Dundas Street among many other venues are well worth a visit.

Restaurants

Glasgow also offers a wide range of restaurants to suit all tastes. Like the hotel listings, the restaurants recommended in this guide have been carefully selected for quality, atmosphere, location and value for money.

The two prices given for each establishment represent a minimum and maximum price for a full meal excluding beverages.

Stravaigin, 28 Gibson St, (basement) G12 8NX; ☎ 0141 334 2665; stravaigin@btinternet.com; £28.95. Basement restaurant with bright murals. A refined instinct for genuinely global cuisine produces surprising but well-prepared combinations – ask about pre-theatre menus.

The Ubiquitous Chip, 12 Ashton Lane G12 8SJ; ☎ 0141 334 5007; mail@ubiquitouschip.co.uk; £21.50-£37.50. A long standing favourite, «The Chip» mixes Scottish and fusion styles. Well known for its glass-roofed courtyard, with a more formal but equally lively warehouse interior.

Dining Room, 41 Byres Rd G11 5RG; ☎ 0141 339 3666; £27.50-£32.95. Split-level dining room with open kitchen facing the street, minimalist décor and unadorned walls. Modern cooking with some Asian influences.

Frango, The Italian Centre, 15 John St G1 1HP; ☎ 0141 552 4433; info@frangorestaurant.co.uk; £13.95-£28. Stylish restaurant with lovely terrace, open all day to diners. Vivid, tiled interior. Separate upstairs room for private functions. Appealing, modern European menus.

La Parmigiana, 447 Great Western Rd, Kelvinbridge G12 8HH; ☎ 0141 334 0686; s.gicovanazzi@btclick.com; £9.50-£31.10. Compact, pleasantly decorated shop conversion with a lively atmosphere and a good local reputation. Obliging, professional service and a sound, authentic Italian repertoire.

No. Sixteen, 16 Byres Rd G11 5JY; ☎ 0141 339 2544; £12.50-£27.25. In the student quarter; small, friendly and personally run. Justly popular for modest prices and a regularly changing, confidently prepared menu: fresh, varied, unfussy.

Bouzy Rouge, 111 West Regent St, G2 2RU; ☎ 0141 221 8804; res@bouzy-rouge.com. £14.95-£26.50. Informal dining in a popular basement restaurant serving modern, Mediterranean-inspired cuisine: candlelit booths and vivid burgundy interior with elaborate metalwork.

Shimla Pinks, 777 Pollokshaws Rd, G41 2AX; ☎ 0141 423 4488; £6.95-£24.85. Simple, modern interior with white walls and contemporary lighting. Sound repertoire of Indian cuisine. A well-run restaurant to south of city. Good value set lunch menu.

Mao, 84 Brunswick St, G1 1ZZ; ☎ 0141 564 5161; info@cafemao.com; £13.50-£22. Eatery located over two floors which are decorated in bright, funky style with vivid, modern colours – broadly themed on Chairman Mao. Thoroughly tasty South East Asian food.

Stravaigin 2, 8 Ruthven Lane, G12 9BG; ☎ 0141 334 7165; stravaigin@btinternet.com; £12.95-£28.95. Lilac painted building tucked away in an alley off Byres Road. Simple and unfussy bistro-style interior. Contemporary menu offering eclectic range of international fare.

For a light meal or afternoon tea visit the delightful **Willow Rooms** at 217 Sauchiehall Street, designed by C R Mackintosh for Miss Cranston.

■ Further reading ■

A Century of the Scottish People 1560-1830 – T C Smout, Fontana Press 1987

Up Oor Close: Memories of Domestic Life in Glasgow Tenements, 1910-45 – Jean Faley, White Cockade 1990

The Scottish Enlightenment: The Scots' Invention of the Modern World – Arthur Herman, Fourth Estate 2003

Great Glasgow Stories – John Burrowes, Mainstream 1998

The Story of Scotland – Nigel Tranter, Lochar Publishing Ltd 1991

Scotland, A New History – Michael Lynch, Pimlico 1992

A Concise History of Scotland – Fitzroy Maclean, Thames & Hudson 2000

The Battle for Scotland – Andrew Marr, Penguin 1995

Scottish Painting 1837 to the Present – William Hardie, Studio Vista 1990

Scottish Art 1460-1990 – Duncan Macmillan, Mainstream Publishing Company (Edinburgh) 1990

Mungo's City: A Glasgow Anthology – Brian D Osborne , Ronald Armstrong, Birlinn 1999

Poetical Works of Robert Burns edited by W & R Chambers Ltd 1990

Reflections on Scotland – Ian Wallace, Jarrold Colour Publications 1988

Scotland, An Anthology – Douglas Dunn, Fontana 1992

Whisky Galore – Compton Mackenzie, Penguin Books 1957

Broths to Bannocks – Catherine Brown, John Murray Ltd 1990

■ Calendar of Events ■

January 25th	**Burns Night**: Burns Suppers to celebrate the birthday of the national poet with haggis as the main dish
March	**'Whuppity Scourie'**: Lanark ceremony banishing winter
May	**Mayfest**
June	**Lanark Lanimer Festival** **Scottish Pipe Bank Championship** **Glasgow International Folk Festival, Jazz Festival**
July-August	**World Pipe Band Champtionship** **Largs Viking Festival**
November-December	**Winterfest**: Christmas lights and ice-skating in the city centre
December 31st	**Hogmanay**, with celebrations based around George Square

INDEX

Director	David Brabis
Series Editor	Mike Brammer
Editorial	Alison Hughes
Picture Editor	Eliane Bailly, Geneviève Corbic
Mapping	Michèle Cana, Alain Baldet
Graphics Coordination	Marie-Pierre Renier
Graphics	Antoine Diemoz-Rosset
Lay-out	Michel Moulin, Alain Fossé
Typesetting	Sophie Rassel and Franck Malagie (NORDCOMPO)
Production	Renaud Leblanc
Marketing	Cécile Petiau, Hervé Binétruy
Sales	John Lewis (UK), Robin Bird (USA)
Public Relations	Gonzague de Jarnac, Paul Cordle

Contact

Michelin Travel Publications
Hannay House
39 Clarendon Road
Watford
Herts
WD17 1JA
United Kingdom
☎ (01923) 205 240
Fax (01923) 205 241
www.ViaMichelin.com
TheGreenGuide-uk@uk.michelin.com

Hannay House, 39 Clarendon Road.
Watford, Herts WD17 1JA, UK
www.ViaMichelin.com
TheGreenGuide-uk@uk.michelin.com

. . . .

MANUFACTURE FRANÇAISE DES PNEUMATIQUES MICHELIN
Société en commandite par actions au capital de 304 000 000 EUR
Place des Carmes-Déchaux – 63 Clermont-Ferrand (France)
R.C.S. Clermont-Fd B 855 200 507

Published in 2004

Front cover:
Glasgow University (S Hughes) – *Clyde Estuary* (Greater Glasgow & Clyde Valley Tourist Board) – *Tinto Hill* (Greater Glasgow & Clyde Valley Tourist Board) – *Detail, The Italian Centre* (S Hughes) – *Café Society* (Greater Glasgow & Clyde Valley Tourist Board)